THE LAW AND AUTONOMOUS VEHICLES

Contemporary Commercial Law

Causation in Insurance Contract Law
Meixian Song

Insurance Law in China
Edited by Johanna Hjalmarsson
and Dingjing Huang

Maritime Law in China: Emerging Issues and Future Developments
Edited by Johanna Hjalmarsson and
Jenny Jingbo Zhang

Illegality in Marine Insurance Law
Feng Wang

Insurance Law Implications of Delay in Maritime Transport
Ayşegül Buğra

Online Arbitration
Faye Fangfei Wang

Double Insurance and Contribution
Nisha Mohamed

The Law and Autonomous Vehicles
Matthew Channon, Lucy McCormick
and Kyriaki Noussia

FIDIC Yellow Book: A Commentary
Ben Beaumont

For more information about this series, please visit: www.routledge.com/Contemporary-Commercial-Law/book-series/CCL

THE LAW AND AUTONOMOUS VEHICLES

MATTHEW CHANNON, LUCY McCORMICK AND KYRIAKI NOUSSIA

informa law
from Routledge

First published 2019
by Informa Law from Routledge
2 Park Square, Milton Park, Abingdon, Oxon OX14 4RN

and by Informa Law from Routledge
605 Third Avenue, New York, NY 10017

First issued in paperback 2020

Informa Law from Routledge is an imprint of the Taylor & Francis Group, an informa business

British Library Cataloguing-in-Publication Data
A catalogue record for this book is available from the British Library

Library of Congress Cataloging-in-Publication Data
Names: Channon, Matthew, author. | McCormick, Lucy, author. | Noussia, Kyriaki, author.
Title: The law and autonomous vehicles / By Matthew Channon, Lucy McCormick and Kyriaki Noussia.
Description: New York, NY: Informa Law from Routledge, 2019. | Series: Contemporary commercial law
Identifiers: LCCN 2018043582 | ISBN 9781138235960 (hbk) | ISBN 9781315268187 (ebk)
Subjects: LCSH: Autonomous vehicles–Law and legislation. | Automated guided vehicle systems–Law and legislation | Automobiles–Automatic control.
Classification: LCC K4034.A98 C53 2019 | DDC 343.09/46–dc23
LC record available at https://lccn.loc.gov/2018043582

ISBN 13: 978-0-367-73195-3 (pbk)
ISBN 13: 978-1-138-23596-0 (hbk)

Typeset in Times New Roman
by codeMantra

CONTENTS

AUTHOR BIOGRAPHIES

Dr Matthew Channon is a Lecturer in Law at the University of Exeter. He presents both nationally and internationally on the law and autonomous vehicles and motor insurance law. Matthew was awarded with an Association Internationale de Droit des Assurances Academic Prize in 2016. He has carried out extensive research in the subject and has contributed to written consultation responses in relation to both the House of Commons and House of Lords.

Lucy McCormick is a commercial barrister at Henderson Chambers. She undertakes a variety of product liability and property damage work, and lectures nationally and internationally on the legal issues arising from autonomous vehicles. Lucy was a finalist for the 2017 CogX Artificial Intelligence award for Industry Analysis.

Dr Kyriaki Noussia is a Senior Lecturer in Law at the University of Exeter. She has expertise on law and technology including insurance and cyber security issues for autonomous vehicles. At the 2018 AIDA World Congress, Kyriaki co-chaired the plenary session on 'New Technologies: Autonomous Vehicles and Robots, Cyber Risks'.

ACKNOWLEDGMENTS

The authors would like to thank a number of people who have provided support throughout the writing process. The authors would like to collectively thank Caroline Church and Amy Jones from Informa Law for all of their assistance and advice in making this book a reality. The authors would further like to thank Professor Rob Merkin QC, Dr Séverine Saintier, Professor Andrea Lista as well as Felix Boon for commenting on drafts of the insurance chapter. Any errors are the authors'.

The authors would further like to thank their family members for their support and encouragement. Matthew would like to thank in particular his fiancée Alison Adams.

This book is up to date as at 31 August 2018. Readers are also referred to the Law Commission consultation paper 'Automated Vehicles: a joint preliminary consultation paper' which was released on 8 November 2018, after the text for this book was finalised.

TABLE OF CASES

United Kingdom

European Court of Justice

Austria

Germany

TABLE OF LEGISLATION

Statutory Instruments

European Union

Regulations

Directives

Other National Laws

Austria

Germany

CHAPTER 1

Introduction

Matthew Channon, Lucy McCormick and Kyriaki Noussia

Introduction

1.1 The history of car making has been one of gradually increasing levels of automation. The first cruise control was marketed in 1958. In 1995, 'adaptive cruise control' was launched, which allowed a vehicle to use sensors to stay a fixed distance from a vehicle in front. By 2010, more advanced functions were being added, such as 'blind spot intervention' and 'active lane keeping assist'. More recently, manufacturers have begun to build on such functions to develop integrated 'motorway assist' systems, to take full control of the vehicle's position and speed whilst driving along a high-speed road, under the supervision of the driver. It is then a relatively small step towards vehicles that do not require the supervision of the driver at all on certain types of roads, and from then on to full automation. It is with the law of such highly and fully automated vehicles that this book is concerned.

Development and testing of autonomous vehicles

1.2 'Driverless' vehicles in one form or another have been demonstrated since the 1920s. For example, in 1926, a vehicle known as the 'Linriccan Wonder' was launched which could be operated by radio impulses from a second vehicle behind it. However, for many decades, as the Computer History Museum puts it, 'real progress was more incremental than revolutionary'.[1] It was not until the mid-1980s that the 'underlying computing and other technologies needed ... became available' for meaningful development in this area.[2] The increasing pace of progress can be seen in the results of the challenges set by the US Defence Advanced Research Projects Agency (DARPA) in the mid-2000s.[3] In 2004, the challenge was to design a vehicle to navigate a 142-mile desert course with a $1 million prize for the winner who managed to complete

1 Computer History Museum, 'Where to? A History of Autonomous Vehicles' (8 May 2014), www.computerhistory.org/atchm/where-to-a-history-of-autonomous-vehicles, accessed 29 August 2018.

2 James M. Anderson et al., *Autonomous Vehicle Technology: A Guide for Policymakers* (RAND Corporation, 2014), 56.

3 Ibid.

the course in less than ten hours.[4] However, the technological hurdles and rugged desert course proved to be too much for the teams' first attempt, and none finished the course – the top-scoring vehicle travelled only 7.5 miles.[5] Yet by the following year, five teams finished the course.[6]

1.3 More recently, the testing of autonomous vehicles has become the focus of substantial commercial investment. For example, Google began testing driverless cars on the streets of the US in 2009 and had driven two million miles up to 2016. More recently, Nissan have begun testing driverless taxis in Japan.[7] The UK government has so far invested millions in research and development,[8] including multiple projects such as:

(a) UK Autodrive – a three-year consortium-led project testing vehicles on roads in Milton Keynes and Coventry;[9]
(b) HumanDrive – a 30-month consortium-led project testing vehicles on a number of different roads in the UK;[10]
(c) Venturer – a three-year research development project funded by both government and industry, trialling vehicles in Bristol and South Gloucestershire;[11] and
(d) Gateway – driverless pods providing a shuttle service around the Greenwich Peninsula which was aimed at understanding the perception and acceptance of such vehicles.[12]

1.4 In 2017, UK Chancellor of the Exchequer Philip Hammond stated that autonomous vehicles are 'going to revolutionise our lives…and the way we work'.[13] Indeed, the technology has many advocates, who cite benefits including greater mobility,[14] fewer road accidents,[15] environmental benefits and economic benefits.

4 DARPA, 'The DARPA Grand Challenge: Ten Years Later' (2014), www.darpa.mil/news-events/2014-03-13, accessed 29 August 2018.

5 Ibid.

6 Ibid.

7 BBC, 'Nissan to trial robo-taxis in Japan' (5 December 2017), www.bbc.co.uk/news/technology-42238112, accessed 29 August 2018.

8 The CCAV state that they have invested £120 million into UK projects with a further £68 million coming from industry; see CCAV, 'UK Connected & Autonomous Vehicle Research & Development Projects 2018' (2018), 8, https://assets.publishing.service.gov.uk/government/uploads/system/uploads/attachment_data/file/725522/ccav-research-and-development-projects.pdf, accessed 31 August 2018.

9 See www.ukautodrive.com, accessed 28 August 2018.

10 See https://humandrive.co.uk/faqs, accessed 28 August 2018.

11 www.venturer-cars.com, accessed 28 August 2018.

12 https://gateway-project.org.uk/about, accessed 31 August 2018.

13 Gwyn Topham, 'Philip Hammond pledges driverless cars by 2021 and warns people to retrain' (*Guardian*, 23 November 2017), www.theguardian.com/world/2017/nov/23/philip-hammond-pledges-driverless-cars-by-2021-and-warns-people-to-retrain, accessed 29 August 2018.

14 Ibid.

15 As noted by the Association of British Insurers (ABI): 'The benefits of driver assistance and automation come from eliminating driver errors that contribute to causing collisions', in ABI and Thatcham Research, 'Regulating Automated Driving: The UK Insurer View' (July 2017), 24. www.mynewsdesk.com/uk/thatcham-research/documents/regulating-automated-driving-a-uk-insurer-view-69167, accessed 16 October 2018.

However, the road to driverless cars is not straightforward, with the safety of these vehicles, and purported benefits,[16] having been called into question. The recent death of a pedestrian during Uber's testing of an autonomous vehicle in Arizona in March 2018 has put such issues into particularly stark focus.[17]

Legal issues and responses

1.5 Legal issues are, of course, at the centre of some of the challenges facing this technology. The UK and a number of other jurisdictions are investigating and implementing legal reforms with a view to smoothing the path for these advances. In February 2015, the UK Department for Transport concluded a detailed review of existing legislation, culminating in the publication of 'The Pathway to Driverless Cars: A detailed review of regulations for automated vehicle technologies'.[18] In July 2015, this was followed by 'The Pathway to Driverless Cars: A Code of Practice for testing', designed to provide non-statutory guidelines for manufacturers and testing organisations when testing autonomous vehicles on public roads.[19] This was followed the same year by the formation of the Centre for Connected and Autonomous Vehicles (CCAV), a joint Department for Business, Energy & Industrial Strategy (BEIS) and Department for Transport (DfT) policy team. In August 2017, the CCAV introduced 'The key principles of vehicle cyber security for connected and automated vehicles', a set of non-statutory principles for use throughout the automotive sector.[20] In March 2018, the government announced the start of a three-year project by the Law Commission of England and Wales and the Scottish Law Commission to undertake a far-reaching review of the UK's legal framework for road-based automated vehicles.[21] Finally, in July 2018, the Automated and Electric Vehicles Act 2018 was given Royal Assent, making provision in relation to the liability of insurers where an accident is caused by an automated vehicle.[22]

1.6 Despite this high level of activity, it is impossible to anticipate every legal issue that will occur, as some will not become evident until more advanced forms of the technology have been introduced and are publicly available. Moreover,

16 See, for example, Patrick Moriarty and Stephen Jia Wang, 'Could automated vehicles reduce transport energy?' 9th International Conference on Applied Energy, ICAE2017, 21–24 August 2017, Cardiff, who state: 'AVs could reduce GHG emissions per vehicle-km, mainly because of the increased fuel efficiency make possible by re-designed lighter vehicles and reduced air friction. However, these gains would probably be swamped by far higher levels of car travel, facilitated by lower perceived time and money costs per km, possible increases in car ownership, and possible loss of public transport patronage', 2112.

17 This was given press attention across the world causing Uber to shut down its self-driving operation in Arizona: 'Uber ends Arizona driverless car programme' (BBC, 23 May 2018), www.bbc.co.uk/news/business-44232536, accessed 29 August 2018.

18 'The Pathway to Driverless Cars: A detailed review of regulations for automated vehicle technologies' (Department for Transport, 2015), www.gov.uk/government/uploads/system/uploads/attachment_data/file/401565/pathway-driverless-cars-main.pdf, accessed 31 August 2018.

19 See Chapter 2.

20 See Chapter 5.

21 See Chapter 7.

22 See Chapter 3.

the breadth of the legal challenges is substantial, encompassing areas of law such as insurance, product liability, cyber security and data protection.

Technology and terminology

1.7 Autonomous vehicles are often described as 'driverless cars' or 'self-driving cars' –the terms are essentially interchangeable. In the industry, they tend to be known by the blanket term 'CAV', which is short for connected and autonomous vehicles. An understanding of the definitions used for describing the level of automation in a particular vehicle is essential in this area. A number of scales have been developed for this, almost all of which concur that 'Level 0' is a vehicle in which the driver is in complete control and 'Level 5' is a fully autonomous vehicle. The most commonly used scale is that developed by the Society of Automotive Engineers (SAE) and known as J3016. This has been adopted by the US Department of Transportation's National Highway Traffic Safety Administration, amongst others. The scale can be summarised as follows:

Table 1.1 Summary of the levels of automation

Level	*Name*	*Definition*
0	No automation	The full-time performance by the human driver of all aspects of the dynamic driving task, even when enhanced by warning or intervention systems.
1	Driver assistance	The driving mode-specific execution by a driver assistance system of either steering or acceleration/deceleration using information about the driving environment and with the expectation that the human driver perform all remaining aspects of the dynamic driving task.
2	Partial automation	The driving mode-specific execution by one or more driver assistance systems of both steering and acceleration/deceleration using information about the driving environment and with the expectation that the human driver perform all remaining aspects of the dynamic driving task.
3	Conditional automation	The driving mode-specific performance by an automated driving system of all aspects of the dynamic driving task with the expectation that the human driver will respond appropriately to a request to intervene.
4	High automation	The driving mode-specific performance by an automated driving system of all aspects of the dynamic driving task, even if a human driver does not respond appropriately to a request to intervene.
5	Full automation	The full-time performance by an automated driving system of all aspects of the dynamic driving task under all roadway and environmental conditions that can be managed by a human driver.

1.8 The SAE levels show that the development of driverless cars is not simply a case of the vehicle having no driver, but rather a development in stages featuring both low and high levels of automation. Lower automation vehicles (up to and including Level 3) require the vehicle user to be monitoring and 'in the loop'. This is assisted driving whereby vehicles undertake some of the functions such as parking, braking and lane assist. Later versions of assisted driving (Level 3) can perform all of the functions in certain situations, although requiring the user to be ready to take back control at any time. Vehicles with higher automation (Levels 4 and 5) will be able to drive with no assistance or monitoring. Hence, even though the term 'driverless cars' is commonly used, this is perhaps not conducive with the reality of their development, and where vehicles are termed 'driverless' it could instead connote a vehicle which has some automated features but continues to require a driver to monitor or assist.

Book structure

1.9 This book is contained in seven chapters (including the present one). Chapter 2 deals with the issue of the legal regime with regards to the testing of autonomous vehicles, in particular the 2015 Code of Practice for testing autonomous vehicles on public roads. Chapter 3 deals with the insurance law regime, particularly in light of the Automated and Electric Vehicles Act 2018. Chapter 4 deals with product liability aspects of autonomous vehicles. Chapter 5 examines the cyber security and data protection challenges for driverless cars, and the approaches undertaken both nationally and internationally to deal with these. Chapter 6 deals with international approaches currently undertaken in relation to autonomous vehicles. Chapter 7 is a wide-ranging consideration of potential future developments in relation to the law of autonomous vehicles.

CHAPTER 2

Testing autonomous vehicles

Lucy McCormick

Introduction

2.1 As with any product, manufacturers must ensure that autonomous vehicles are subjected to appropriate quality control and testing before they become commercially available. As the risk presented by vehicles is high, the standard of testing expected will be correspondingly stringent.[1]

2.2 Most autonomous vehicles will undertake extensive testing in simulations as well as on closed roads or test tracks. However, ultimately testing on public roads will be necessary. Indeed, testing on public roads in multiple jurisdictions is likely to be prudent, given the potential for local variations in driving conventions and hazards.[2]

2.3 As to the legal status of testing on public roads, the UK government conducted a review of existing legislation in 2015, concluding that:

> Real-world testing of automated technologies is possible in the UK today, providing a test driver is present and takes responsibility for the safe operation of the vehicle; and that the vehicle can be used compatibly with road traffic law.[3]

2.4 In reaching this conclusion, the Department for Transport carried out a detailed review of various provisions, including the Road Vehicles (Construction and Use) Regulations 1986. Notably, Regulation 104 provides that:

> No person shall drive or cause or permit any other person to drive, a motor vehicle on a road if he is in such a position that he cannot have proper control of the vehicle or have a full view of the road and traffic ahead.

However, the view taken by the Department for Transport was that this Regulation 'would seem to be satisfied when the test driver has access to all necessary controls, even if not actively operating them, and is able to clearly see the road ahead'.[4]

1 Cf. *Lunt v Khelifa* [2002] EWCA Civ 801, [20] *per* Latham LJ: 'this court has consistently imposed on the drivers of cars a high burden to reflect the fact that a car is potentially a dangerous weapon'.

2 For example: in cold climates automated vehicles can encounter difficulties when road markings are obscured by snow; in Greece (unlike the rest of Europe) road users entering a roundabout have right of way.

3 'The Pathway to Driverless Cars: A detailed review of regulations for automated vehicle technologies' (Department for Transport, February 2015), 8, www.gov.uk/government/uploads/system/uploads/attachment_data/file/401565/pathway-driverless-cars-main.pdf, accessed 31 August 2018.

4 Ibid., 10.23.

2.5 The legal status of testing on public roads in the UK is in fact relatively unusual, compared with other jurisdictions. In many countries, primary legislation is necessary to enable testing of autonomous vehicles. In addition, many countries are subject to the 1968 Vienna Convention on Road Traffic, which until March 2016 required that 'every moving vehicle or combination of vehicles shall have a driver' and that 'every driver shall at all times, be able to control his vehicle'. This therefore arguably precluded the testing of automated vehicles in such countries.[5] This was not an obstacle in the UK, which had signed but not ratified the Vienna Convention.

2.6 Road users owe a general duty of care to other road users, and will be liable in negligence if breach of that duty causes damage. During testing, the test driver will be under a duty of care to other road users in the normal way. The standard of care expected is that of a skilled, experienced, careful driver making no errors of judgment.[6]

2.7 During testing, if the vehicle is in manual mode, the test driver would be as culpable as a standard driver for any collisions. If the vehicle is in an automatic mode, it is anticipated that the position would remain the same. This is because a test driver ought to be continually monitoring the vehicle and able to take over active control of the movement and direction of the vehicle at any moment.[7]

2.8 Under the principles of vicarious liability, the employer of the test driver would be responsible for the actions of its employee.[8] As a result, it is not overly significant – from the perspective of a third party involved in a collision – whether said collision is caused by a lapse of judgment by the test driver or by a failure in the design of the test by the test operator. Of course, if the failure of the automated technology is at fault, there is also the potential for a claim against the manufacturer; probably in the form of a claim from the test driver or testing organisation in breach of contract/negligence for a contribution.

2.9 Generally speaking, the Consumer Protection Act 1987 will not be relevant in the context of the testing of autonomous vehicles. This is because the CPA 1987 provides a defence for defendants who have not 'supplied' defective products.[9] Given that it is likely that the automated vehicle will remain the property of the manufacturer or testing organisation throughout the testing process, CPA 1987 liability is unlikely to arise.

5 This includes most of Europe and several central Asian and South American countries, but notably not the USA or China.

6 See *Nettleship v Weston* [1971] 2 QB 691, in which it was held that the same standard of care should be applied to a learner driver as to an experienced driver. The government is presently considering whether it might in future be appropriate to provide that the standard of driving to be expected from an autonomous vehicle is higher than that of a human driver.

7 'The Pathway to Driverless Cars: A Code of Practice for testing' (Department for Transport, July 2015), 5.13, www.gov.uk/government/publications/automated-vehicle-technologies-testing-code-of-practice, accessed 27 August 2018.

8 Vicarious liability is concerned with whether one person should be held responsible for the acts of another. In an employment context, the general test is whether the tort was 'so closely connected with his employment that it would be fair and just to hold the [employer] vicariously liable' (*per* Lord Steyn in *Lister v Hesley Hall* [2001] UKHL 22).

9 Consumer Protection Act 1987, s 4(1)(b).

2.10 Following on from its regulatory review, in July 2015 the UK Government issued a document entitled 'The Pathway to Driverless Cars: A Code of Practice for testing' ('the Code of Practice').[10] This provided specific guidance on testing automated vehicle technologies on public roads or in other public places in the UK. The Code of Practice addresses many practical aspects of testing, from test driver qualifications to liaison with local authorities.

2.11 In addition to the Code of Practice, developers may also wish to consider the general legislative requirements relating to the use of prototype vehicles on UK roads.

Code of Practice for Testing

2.12 The Code of Practice provides guidance for those wishing to conduct testing of highly or fully automated vehicle technologies on public roads or in other public places in the UK. It makes recommendations on how to maintain safety and minimise potential risks.

2.13 The Code of Practice applies to the testing of a wide range of vehicles, from smaller automated pods and shuttles, through to cars, vans and heavy-duty vehicles. The Code is not intended to apply to the testing and development of ADAS[11] or tests carried out on private test tracks or other areas not accessible by the public. The guidelines may nonetheless be of assistance in considering good practice in these situations.

2.14 The Code of Practice is non-statutory. It was a deliberate decision by the UK government to deal with this by guidance rather than through legislation or a permit system. As was said in the regulatory review which preceded the Code of Practice: 'A Code of Practice will be quicker to establish, more flexible and less onerous for those wishing to engage in testing than the regulatory approach being followed in other countries, notably in the US.'[12] Despite its non-statutory status, the Code of Practice would be taken into account in any litigation. It has been said by the Department for Transport that

> failure to follow guidance in a Code of Practice would be a clear indicator of negligence. A Code of Practice that reflects good and responsible practice with regard to the safety of other road users would carry considerable weight on any issue of liability.[13]

---

10 'The Pathway to Driverless Cars: A Code of Practice for testing' (Department for Transport, July 2015). www.gov.uk/government/publications/automated-vehicle-technologies-testing-code-of-practice, accessed 27 August 2018.

11 Advanced Driver Assistance Systems – i.e. advanced technologies that fall short of offering an automated mode which allows the driver to 'disengage' from the driving task.

12 'The Pathway to Driverless Cars: A detailed review of regulations for automated vehicle technologies' (Department for Transport, February 2015), 14, www.gov.uk/government/uploads/system/uploads/attachment_data/file/401565/pathway-driverless-cars-main.pdf, accessed 31 August 2018.

13 Ibid., 15. See also the comments in 'The Pathway to Driverless Cars: A Code of Practice for testing' (Department for Transport; July 2015), 1.5, that 'Failure to follow the Code may be relevant to liability in any legal proceedings. Similarly, compliance with the Code does not guarantee immunity from liability in such circumstances', www.gov.uk/government/publications/automated-vehicle-technologies-testing-code-of-practice, accessed 27 August 2018.

As such, this is similar to the status of the Highway Code.[14]

2.15 The Code of Practice has been generally well received, and has been adopted as a starting point for autonomous vehicle testing by other countries, notably Belgium.

2.16 Key points from the Code of Practice include:

(a) organisations wishing to test automated vehicles on public roads or in other public places will need to ensure that the vehicles have first successfully completed in-house testing on closed roads or test tracks;
(b) any vehicle on a public road will require a 'driver' to be present, whether or not the vehicle is in an automated mode. Testing in other places such as pavements or pedestrian areas will require as a minimum the oversight of a test operator who can apply an emergency stop control from outside the vehicle;
(c) the controls should give the test driver a clear indication of whether the vehicle is in manual or automated mode, and should allow the driver to quickly retake control of the vehicle when necessary;
(d) vehicles will need to have appropriate levels of security built into them to manage the risk of hacking;[15]
(e) automated vehicles under test should be fitted with a 'black box' data recording device for analysis in case of an incident; and
(f) it is recommended that test drivers should continue to maintain gaze directions appropriate for normal driving, to avoid unnerving other road users.

2.17 Such specific recommendations on testing protocol are the most distinctive feature of the Code of Practice. However, the Code of Practice also draws together a number of pieces of practical guidance in relation to insurance, driver qualifications, liaison with local authorities and emergency services and so on. Some of these are considered below.

2.18 The Code of Practice is intended to be subject to periodic review, to ensure that it keeps pace with best practice and takes into account experience from testing. Although no date has yet been announced for a second edition of the Code of Practice, this is widely anticipated to be released in late 2018/early 2019.

14 See s 28(7) of the Road Traffic Act 1988 to the effect that 'A failure on the part of a person to observe a provision of the Highway Code shall not of itself render that person liable to criminal proceedings of any kind but any such failure may in any proceedings (whether civil or criminal, and including proceedings for an offence under the Traffic Acts, the Public Passenger Vehicles Act 1981 or sections 18 to 23 of the Transport Act 1985) be relied upon by any party to the proceedings as tending to establish or negative any liability which is in question in those proceedings'. See also *Wakeling v McDonagh* [2007] EWHC 1201 (QB), [24], in which Judge Mackie QC held, that 'Any breach of the Highway Code is relevant but not determinative', and *Goad v Butcher* [2011] EWCA Civ 158, [9], in which Moore-Bick LJ held that 'A failure to observe the Highway Code might be evidence of negligence causing or contributing to a road traffic accident, but whether it was would depend very much on the circumstances in which the question was committed and who the claimant was'.

15 See Chapter 5.

General considerations for testing

Road traffic laws

2.19 Vehicles under test on public roads must obey all relevant road traffic laws. It is the responsibility of testing organisations to satisfy themselves that all tests planned to be undertaken comply with all relevant existing laws and that the vehicles involved are roadworthy, meet all relevant vehicle requirements, and can be used in a way that is compatible with existing UK road traffic law.

2.20 In particular, vehicles under test must comply with Regulation 100 of the Road Vehicles (Construction and Use) Regulations 1986 to the effect that (*inter alia*):

> A motor vehicle…and all parts and accessories of such vehicle…shall at all times be in such condition…that no danger is caused or is likely to be caused to any person in or on the vehicle or trailer or on a road.

2.21 Also of note is Regulation 110, which provides that 'No person shall drive a motor vehicle on a road if he is using: (a) a hand-held mobile telephone; or (b) a hand-held device of a kind specified in paragraph (4)', being 'a device, other than a two-way radio, which performs an interactive communication function by transmitting and receiving data'.[16] By virtue of Section 41D of the Road Traffic Act 1988, to do so is an offence. As such, if it is the intention that data be recorded in real time during testing on a tablet computer or laptop, the testing organisation will need to employ a test assistant as passenger, in addition to the test driver.

Insurance requirements

2.22 The statutory requirements on the holding of insurance will apply whilst a vehicle is being tested. Anyone conducting tests of automated vehicles on public roads or in other public places must therefore hold appropriate insurance.[17]

2.23 Unlike some other jurisdictions, there is no requirement in the UK for a surety bond.

Driver qualifications

2.24 Under current legislation, a person who holds a full category B (car) driving licence is authorised to drive any car. There are no specific requirements beyond this which would be necessary for a test driver to operate a

16 Note that Regulation 110 was amended in June 2018 by the Road Vehicles (Construction and Use) (Amendment) Regulations 2018/592 reg. 2(2) to add a new paragraph 5A to clarify that the use of remote control parking technologies is permissible in certain circumstances. See para 7.5.

17 For more information about insurance and automated vehicles, see Chapter 3.

highly or fully automated vehicle. Testing organisations should ensure that test drivers and operators hold the appropriate driving licence. For the avoidance of doubt, a test driver must hold the appropriate category of licence for the vehicle under test, even if it is being tested in a fully autonomous mode.

2.25 In practice, additional training for test drivers and operators is likely to be desirable for the early stages of testing on public roads. Drivers with several years' experience of driving the relevant category of vehicle are to be preferred. It may be prudent to select test drivers who have already completed advanced driving qualifications, such as those offered by the Institute of Advanced Motorists or in the course of police/military training. In any event, test drivers should be offered specific training in relation to the vehicle under test and its potential limitations. Training in the process for transitioning between conventional manual control and an automated mode will be particularly important. Such testing would normally be carried out on a closed track, prior to use on public roads.

2.26 For the final stages of testing, it may be appropriate to use test drivers who are representative of an 'average driver' – that is to say without special qualifications. Such testing would need to be particularly closely monitored.

Risk assessments

2.27 It would also be appropriate for a testing organisation to conduct a detailed risk assessment of any proposed tests. This will involve identifying the relevant hazards, considering who might be harmed and how, deciding on precautions, and keeping the assessment regularly updated. Whilst the use of a qualified health and safety professional to carry out the assessment is not strictly necessary, it is likely to be prudent in this context.

2.28 The identification of risks will be highly fact specific. However, two known areas of concern are (i) the transition between conventional manual control and an automated mode and (ii) the risk of lapses of concentration during long periods monitoring automated equipment.[18] Testing organisations may wish to set limits on the amount of time that test drivers spend on such a role per day. They should also give extensive thought as to how to indicate clearly to a test driver which mode the vehicle is in, and make it straightforward to implement a manual override at any time.

Liaison with local authorities and emergency services

2.29 Testing organisations should consider the need to engage with the relevant transport and highway authorities with responsibility for the areas in which the tests will be conducted.

18 K. Naughton, 'Ford's Dozing Engineers Side with Google in Full Autonomy Push', Bloomberg (17 February 2017), www.bloomberg.com/news/articles/2017-02-17/ford-s-dozing-engineers-side-with-google-in-full-autonomy-push, accessed 27 August 2018.

2.30 Depending on the nature of the test, the authorities may consider custom signage appropriate. If so, this may take some time to authorise as non-standard signage requires the approval of the Secretary of State for Transport. It is a general principle of road design that too many signs can be a problem for road users due to 'sign overload' and distraction, so only signs that are considered truly necessary will be approved.

2.31 Moreover, it is recommended that those wishing to conduct testing of highly and fully automated vehicles on public roads or in other public places should engage with the local emergency services. This should include, where possible, establishing a single point of contact with local police and fire services to facilitate cooperation in the event of an investigation. The availability of technical advice to the emergency services should also be discussed and agreed so that those attending an incident can be aware of any unusual features of automated vehicles.[19] Testing organisations should also consider providing vehicle registration numbers of the vehicles under test to the local police.

Legislative requirements for prototype road vehicles

2.32 In normal circumstances, all vehicles used on the public road have to comply with the Road Vehicles (Construction and Use) Regulations 1986, the Road Vehicles Authorised Weight Regulations 1998 and the Road Vehicles Lighting Regulations 1989.

2.33 However, designers and manufacturers may well wish to use prototype vehicles or equipment on public roads which do not comply with regulations. In these circumstances, they can have recourse to Articles 36 and 37 of the Road Vehicles (Authorisation of Special Types) (General) Order 2003.

2.34 Under the 2003 Order, certain exemptions from the Road Vehicles (Construction and Use) Regulations 1986 and the Road Vehicles Lighting Regulations 1989 are available for particular vehicles identified at Article 36 (1) as follows:

> (c) any new or improved type of motor vehicle or trailer which is constructed for tests or trials;
> (d) any motor vehicle or trailer which is equipped with new or improved equipment;
> (e) any motor vehicle or trailer which is equipped with new or improved types of equipment.[20]

2.35 By Article 37, the authorisation requirements which apply to vehicles falling within such categories are specified in Articles 38–40 (length; width;

19 For example, Waymo (the automated vehicles branch of Google) provided California law enforcement with instructions on how to immobilise its vehicles; this indicated that opening one door would prevent the autonomous car from moving, www.cnbc.com/2018/05/14/alphabet-waymo-tells-police-how-to-break-in-disable-self-driving-cars.html, accessed 27 August 2018.

20 The Authorised Weight Regulations apply in their entirety to prototype vehicles. A prototype is not allowed to exceed the legal axle or vehicle weight limits.

weight) and Schedule 11. Schedule 11 explains that a relevant vehicle may only be used on roads for testing, demonstration or proceeding to, or returning from, a manufacturer or repairer for construction, repair or overhaul.

2.36 Notwithstanding any exemption, by Schedule 4(4) a relevant vehicle must not be used in such a way as to cause a danger of injury to any person by reason of:

(a) the condition of the vehicle, its accessories or equipment;
(b) the purpose for which it is used;
(c) the number of passengers carried by it;
(d) the manner in which such passengers are carried;
(e) the weight, position or distribution of any load carried on the vehicle; or
(f) the manner in which any such load is secured.[21]

21 For further information, see 'Prototype road vehicles – Construction Requirements' (Department for Transport, September 2015), www.gov.uk/government/publications/prototype-vehicles, accessed 27 August 2018.

CHAPTER 3

Insurance

Matthew Channon

Introduction

3.1 Third-party motor insurance for conventional vehicles is compulsory in the United Kingdom (UK) under the Road Traffic Act 1988 (RTA 1988).[1] Where a person is injured as a result of another's use of a vehicle, insurance is provided to ensure compensation of that injured person.[2] However, adapting the RTA 1988 to cater for the absence of driver control in autonomous vehicles has been a significant challenge, as the Act has always been focussed on conventional vehicles. The most significant incompatibility between the RTA 1988 and autonomous vehicles was[3] the requirement for third-party insurance in relation to the vehicle user and not the vehicle.[4] Consequently, there was no compulsory requirement under the RTA 1988 for the vehicle manufacturer to have insurance, necessary to ensure compensation when the vehicle is at fault. Moreover, the users of at-fault vehicles were not protected.[5]

3.2 The UK has sought to solve these incompatibilities through the introduction of a new system for autonomous vehicles within the Automated and Electric Vehicles Act 2018 (AEVA 2018). The Act is a broad piece of legislation, which is not designed to be all encompassing.

3.3 This chapter will focus on the insurance law challenges faced by the introduction of autonomous vehicles and the solution developed by the UK through the AEVA 2018. Whilst the focus of this chapter is very much in the present, it

1 Section 143 (1) RTA 1988, insurance is now also compulsory for autonomous vehicles due to the Automated and Electric Vehicles Act 2018 (Schedule 1 paragraph 19 (2)).

2 Historically, drivers who could not afford compensation for accidents were known as the 'man of straw', and were the ultimate reason behind introducing compulsory third-party insurance in the Road Traffic Act 1930. See, for example, Earl Russell's Bill, Motor Vehicles Compulsory Insurance Bill House of Lords Debate, 15 July 1925, Volume 62, CC76–88, 87. Note that the term 'conventional' is used throughout this chapter as a reference to vehicles which are not autonomous; this includes vehicles which are at the lower end of automation (advanced driver assistance systems).

3 The past tense is used here to connote the situation pre-AEVA 2018, whilst recognising that the AEVA 2018 comes into force 'on whatever day or days the Secretary of State appoints by regulations', Section 21(2)(a) AEVA 2018.

4 As noted by Lord Denning in *Hardy v Motor Insurers' Bureau* [1964] 2 QB 745, 760: 'The policy of insurance which a motorist is required by statute to take out must cover any liability which may be incurred by him arising out of the use of the vehicle by him.'

5 Unless 'comprehensive' cover is purchased.

is important to detail where there are gaps in the Act which will require future exploration either via the legislature or the courts. It is important to note that cyber security and insurance are not mentioned in this chapter and instead are discussed in the cyber security/data protection chapter later.

Conventional motor insurance law

3.4 There is already in place a system of compulsory insurance for use of conventional vehicles in the UK.[6] Whilst it is likely that there will be some reform to motor insurance, to ensure compatibility with autonomous vehicles, much of the current regulation will remain and apply to autonomous vehicles in the government's attempts to 'supplement'[7] the current legal framework.

3.5 Under the third-party compulsory insurance framework for conventional vehicles within the RTA 1988, it is a criminal offence[8] to use[9] a conventional motor vehicle[10] on a 'road or other public place',[11] without an adequate policy of insurance.[12] Insurance must cover road users and passengers[13] in case of an accident[14] caused by or arising out of the use of the vehicle.[15] There are a number of exemptions from insurance within Section 144 RTA 1988 and securities can be held instead of insurance policies (Section 143(1)(a)). In cases where the driver is insured, the responsible driver's insurer is under a duty to compensate victims for personal injury or damage to their property.[16] There are a number of statutory limitations on cover – for example, the insurer is not required to cover for damage to the vehicle which caused the

6 Contained in the RTA 1988.

7 'Pathway to driverless cars: Consultation on proposals to support Advanced Driver Assistance Systems and Automated Vehicles: Government Response' (Centre for Connected and Autonomous Vehicles 2017), [3.11], https://assets.publishing.service.gov.uk/government/uploads/system/uploads/attachment_data/file/581577/pathway-to-driverless-cars-consultation-response.pdf, accessed 31 August 2018.

8 Section 143 RTA 1988.

9 'Causing' or 'permitting' use of a vehicle without insurance is also an offence (Section 143(1)(b) RTA 1988). 'Use' will be discussed later in the chapter.

10 Section 185 provides a definition of motor vehicle which is a 'mechanically propelled vehicle intended or adapted for use on roads'.

11 As noted in *Harrison v Hill* 1932 JC 13, 16: 'What is meant is neither (at one extreme) that the public has a positive right of its own to access, nor (at the other extreme) that there exists no physical obstruction, of greater or less impenetrability, against physical access by the public; but that the public actually and legally enjoys access to it.'

12 Note that under Section 144(1) RTA 1988 this does not apply to a person who deposits for security the sum of £15,000 with the Accountant-General of the Supreme Court.

13 The requirement for insurance to cover injury to passengers was introduced by the Motor Vehicle (Passenger Insurance) Act 1971.

14 Section 143 RTA 1988. 'Accident' is given a wide definition in third-party motor insurance law to include deliberately caused damage; see *Charlton v Fisher* [2002] QB 578.

15 These terms will be defined later in the chapter.

16 Ward LJ in *Bristol Alliance Ltd Partnership v Williams* [2013] QB 806, [34]: '(1) that "a certificate of insurance has been delivered under section 147" (section 151); (2) that "a judgment to which this subsection applies is obtained" (section 151(1)); (3) that the judgment relates "to a liability with respect to any matter where liability with respect to that matter is required to be covered by a policy of insurance under section 145" (section 151(2)); and (4) that the liability is "covered by the terms of the policy...to which the certificate relates" (section 151(2)(a)).'

accident.[17] Where a claimant's negligence was a contributory cause of their loss, the law[18] allows for a reduction in any damages awarded to reflect the level of that contributory fault. Where the driver is uninsured or untraced, the third-party victim may have a claim against the Motor Insurers' Bureau (MIB) under the MIB's Uninsured or Untraced Drivers' Agreements.[19]

3.6 Insurers' duty to compensate is subject to a number of restrictions such as through the use of exclusion clauses[20] (Sections 148 and 151 RTA) and through the insureds' non-disclosure.[21] The use of these defences, however, does not equal an absence of compensation for third-party victims, as claims are picked up by the insurer[22] in conjunction with the MIB Agreements.[23]

3.7 Further, both the Insurance Act 2015 and the Consumer Insurance Disclosure and Representations Act 2012 (CIDRA) are not aimed specifically towards motor insurance but effects all insurance policies.[24] The Insurance Act 2015 deals with, *inter alia*, warranties,[25] fraudulent claims[26] and good faith.[27]

3.8 Finally, UK motor insurance is regulated heavily by the EU Sixth Consolidated Motor Insurance Directive,[28] codifying the previous Motor Insurance Directives. The Directive's purpose is to harmonise motor insurance law across the EU, ensuring that a high standard of protection is maintained for accident victims, regardless of where the accident occurs. The Directives regulate many key areas of motor insurance, including the removal of border checks,[29] compensation schemes,[30] exclusion clauses,[31] the single premium,[32] and scope of compulsory insurance (where the vehicle is insured).[33] The Directive makes it easier for an individual to claim in terms of cross-border accidents, whereby claims can be made by the victim in their Member State of

17 This is will be discussed in more detail later; Section 145(4)(c) RTA 1988.

18 Law Reform (Contributory Negligence) Act 1945.

19 Motor Insurers Bureau, 'Uninsured Drivers' Agreement' (2015); also Motor Insurers' Bureau, 'Untraced Drivers Agreement' (2017). The MIB will be discussed later in this chapter.

20 See *Bristol Alliance Ltd Partnership v Williams* [2013] QB 806.

21 For non-disclosure see Section 152 (2).

22 Under Article 75 of the MIB's Articles of Association. See Motor Insurers' Bureau, 'Articles of Association of Motor Insurers' Bureau' (2018), www.mib.org.uk/media/423529/mib-articles-of-association-19-july-2018.pdf, accessed 28 August 2018.

23 Motor Insurers Bureau, 'Uninsured Drivers' Agreement' (2015); also Motor Insurers' Bureau, 'Untraced Drivers Agreement' (2017).

24 This is subject to the split between consumer and business insurance. Most provisions of the Insurance Act 2015 are aimed at non-consumer insurance, whereas CIDRA is aimed at consumer insurance.

25 Sections 9–11, part three Insurance Act 2015.

26 Sections 12 and 13 Insurance Act 2015.

27 Section 14 Insurance Act 2015.

28 Directive 2009/103/EC of the European Parliament and of the Council relating to insurance against civil liability in respect of the use of motor vehicles, and the enforcement of the obligation to insure against such liability [2009], OJ L 263.

29 Ibid., Article 4.

30 Ibid., Article 10.

31 Ibid., Article 13.

32 Ibid., Article 14.

33 Ibid., Article 1.

residence against a claims representative,[34] meaning that claims can be made under procedures that they may be more accustomed to.[35] Of course, with the UK's imminent departure from the EU at the time of writing,[36] uncertainty exists as to the arrangements in place in relation to both conventional and autonomous vehicles.

Insurance reform

3.9 The two core insurance law issues which were going to be faced in relation to autonomous vehicles have been the subject of significant discussion and attracted significant government interest. The Centre for Connected and Autonomous Vehicles (CCAV) has consulted[37] on ways to address these issues and ensure an insurance system which is compatible for the introduction of the technology.

Incompatibility of the current Road Traffic Act 1988

3.10 The system of conventional motor insurance through the RTA 1988 is incompatible with the introduction of autonomous vehicles, notably at Levels 4 and 5 of the Society of Automotive Engineers taxonomy.[38] Whereas with vehicles of low automation, the user of the vehicle is required to monitor and, if necessary, take over control of the vehicle, higher automation vehicles allow the user to disengage with the driving task.[39]

3.11 In the UK, the driver is required to be covered by insurance for their use of the vehicle;[40] the insurer will then compensate the accident victim. Although manufacturers are liable for product defects under the existing product liability framework[41] as it currently stands, there is no requirement for manufacturers to take out insurance. Consequently, as noted by the CCAV, 'there is a risk of consumer confusion'.[42] For example, it is likely that the manufacturer would have to be taken to court[43] for compensation to be paid.

3.12 Another significant weakness is that even though the 'driver' of the responsible vehicle essentially becomes a victim if the autonomous vehicle

34 Ibid., see Articles 20–26 of the Directive. For example, Article 21 sets out responsibilities and powers of the claims representative.

35 Ibid., Recital 34.

36 The UK departure date of the EU is set to be 29 March 2019.

37 'Pathway to Driverless Cars: Proposals to support advanced driver assistance systems and automated vehicle technologies' (Centre for Connected and Autonomous Vehicles, July 2016), https://assets.publishing.service.gov.uk/government/uploads/system/uploads/attachment_data/file/536365/driverless-cars-proposals-for-adas-and_avts.pdf, accessed 31 August 2018.

38 See Chapter 1 for Society of Automotive Engineer levels.

39 As will be noted later, these vehicles may be able to transcend more than one level, i.e. capable of driving themselves in some situations but not others.

40 *Hardy v Motor Insurers' Bureau* (n 4), 760.

41 Consumer Protection Act 1987.

42 CCAV, 'Pathway to Driverless Cars' (n 37), [2.7].

43 Ibid.

malfunctions, they are not protected for injury or damage[44] to their vehicle or for personal injury to themselves, unless they purchase additional insurance (known as 'comprehensive' coverage). This is because there is no requirement under conventional motor insurance law for the insurer to compensate first parties.

Product liability insurance

3.13 The CCAV's consultation introduced two models to alleviate difficulties faced with the RTA's incompatibility,[45] with most focus on the introduction of product liability insurance as a solution. A product liability approach ensures that both manufacturer and driver liability are covered by insurance, with the owner of the vehicle ensuring that a separate insurance policy is taken out to cover the manufacturer's liability.[46] Where malfunction of the vehicle is the cause of an accident, the product liability policy would be activated and the product liability insurer would compensate. The additional policy would also cover injuries to the user of the not-at-fault vehicle.[47] There are, however, obvious difficulties with a product liability approach due to the absence of protection for accident victims in certain circumstances. This is therefore contradictory to the purpose of motor insurance, which is currently in place to ensure that the victim of an accident is compensated, and not at mercy of the driver's inability to pay.[48] The product liability insurance system would have significant limits. For example, claims can only be made under product liability during the first ten years of a vehicle's lifespan.[49]

3.14 There are a number of defences available for a manufacturer's insurer to use under product liability such as the 'state of the art' defence, allowing the manufacturer to avoid liability if the defect could not have been discovered in light of technological knowledge at the time.[50] Autonomous vehicle technology is advancing gradually and it is likely that a number of stages of the vehicle will be present at the same time. Another critical issue, it is submitted, with regard to a product liability approach is where there are two separate insurers, one for the vehicle and another for the driver. This would be complex

44 Section 145(4)(c) RTA 1988 states 'the policy shall not…be required…to cover liability in respect of damage to the vehicle'.

45 The other proposed solution was the 'first party insurance model'. This was criticised by some in the insurance industry as an impracticable model to follow. See Axa UK, 'Pathway to Driverless Cars: Proposals to Support Advanced Driver Assistance Systems and Automated Vehicle Technology' (8 September 8 2016), 6, https://assets.publishing.service.gov.uk/government/uploads/system/uploads/attachment_data/file/536365/driverless-cars-proposals-for-adas-and_avts.pdf, accessed 30 August 2018.

46 CCAV Pathway to Driverless Cars (n 37), [2.9].

47 Ibid.

48 This was discussed significantly in *Gardner Respondent v Moore and Another Appellants* [1984] AC 548, 555.

49 'Pathway to driverless cars: Government Response' (n 7), [3.09].

50 Section 4(1)(e) Consumer Protection Act 1987.

for the injured party to navigate, due to the need to determine whether it was the vehicle or the driver (and their respective insurers) that was liable.

The Automated and Electric Vehicles Act

3.15 The AEVA 2018[51] passed royal assent in July 2018;[52] however, under Section 21(1) of the Act, this will come into force 'whatever day or days the Secretary of State appoints by regulations', which will be through a statutory instrument.[53] The Act introduces a 'single insurer model' which covers accidents caused by both the user of the vehicle and the autonomous vehicle technology, providing victims (including the driver) with routes to compensation.

Definitions

Automated vehicle

3.16 Under Section 1(1) AEVA 2018, the Secretary of State must compose and keep up to date a list of 'automated vehicles' in the UK. The AEVA 2018 provides that an 'automated vehicle' is (in the Secretary of State's opinion) 'designed or adapted to be capable, in at least some circumstances or situations, of safely driving themselves' (Section 1(1)(a)) and 'may lawfully be used when driving themselves, in at least some circumstances or situations, on roads or other public places in Great Britain' (Section 1(1)(b)).

3.18 This definition, due to the requirement of the vehicle not needing monitoring or control, connotes higher levels of automation (Levels 4 and 5 of the Society of Automotive Engineer levels[54]). It seems therefore that there is an exclusion from the Act of lower automation 'driver assistance systems' which will remain under the remit of the RTA 1988 regime. However, as noted by the Faculty of Actuaries (FOA), 'even though the driver remains in the loop, it does not seem far-fetched to imagine that a malfunction of the assisted technology could cause an accident that is hard for the driver to control'.[55] In the situation noted by the FOA, accident victims would likely recover under product liability laws[56] directly against the manufacturer[57] or attempt to recover against the driver's insurer under the RTA 1988. The at-fault vehicle

51 Note that the Act contains provisions on both 'automated' and 'electric' vehicles. This chapter is only concerned with the former.

52 This was a continuation of the previous Vehicle Technology and Aviation Bill, which failed due to the dissolution of Parliament for a general election in June 2017. The AEVA 2018 remained similar to VTAB, apart from a couple of significant alterations (which will be discussed later).

53 Section 21(3) AEVA 2018.

54 See autonomous vehicle levels in Chapter 1 of this book.

55 Faculty of Actuaries, 'Written evidence submitted by the Institute and Faculty of Actuaries (AEVB 30)' (14 November 2017), 2, https://publications.parliament.uk/pa/cm201719/cmpublic/automated/memo/aevb30.pdf, accessed 29 August 2018.

56 Section 2(1) Consumer Protection Act 1987.

57 As noted in the product liability discussion in paras 3.14–3.15, defences are available to manufacturers.

user, on the other hand, would only have a potential remedy against the product manufacturer.[58]

3.17 The term 'in some situations' within the definition almost certainly means that vehicles need not be fully automated in all situations. The reality is that the development of fully autonomous vehicles without need for a steering wheel is further away.[59] The legislature has therefore wisely covered a potential gap with vehicles that were generally of lower automation but with some limited higher automation potential without the need for driver monitoring.

3.19 Nevertheless, the vehicle's driving needs to be 'safe'. The Act does not provide a safety benchmark such as in comparison to the standard required of human drivers, although comparing safety to the standard of drivers is problematic.[60] As noted by Schellekens, '[a] problem may be that there is not one human driver that is equal to another human driver'.[61] Instead, Schellekens notes, statistics could be used to determine whether the vehicle causes fewer accidents than cars driven by humans.[62] Another formulation as noted by Schellekens, is that the vehicle 'should be safer than the best human driver',[63] which does not mean that the vehicle does not have accidents but that even the best driver could not have prevented those accidents either.[64]

3.20 Some comparator in law for the term 'safety' could be through Regulation 2 of the General Product Safety Regulations 2005, which states that a 'safe product' is one that:

> under normal or reasonably foreseeable conditions of use including duration and, where applicable, putting into service, installation and maintenance requirements, does not present any risk or only the minimum risks compatible with the product's use, considered to be acceptable and consistent with a high level of protection for the safety and health of persons.

3.21 This definition clearly has a high threshold in terms of product safety, whilst recognising that there will be circumstances in which the product will not require safety as a matter of fulling the provision – that is, where as noted in the General Product Safety Regulations 2005 the use is not 'reasonably foreseeable'. Undoubtedly, autonomous vehicles are going to be used in ways

58 As noted in this chapter at para 3.12, insurance is only compulsory under the RTA 1988 to cover for third parties.

59 David Wong provided an answer in evidence to House of Commons Public Bill Committee that 'As to when those level 5 vehicles without steering wheels are capable of performing end-to-end journeys…that is anybody's guess. That will probably be some time in the 2030s.' See Public Bill Committee, *Automated and Electric Vehicles Bill* (Tuesday 31 October 2017 (afternoon) second sitting, 43).

60 Maurice Schellekens, 'Self-driving cars and the chilling effect of liability law' (2015) *Computer Law & Security Review*, Vol. 31, No. 4, 506–517, [4.2.2].

61 Ibid., 510.

62 Ibid., 510.

63 Ibid.

64 Ibid.

not envisaged by the manufacturer, and a substantial issue for the Secretary of State will be deciding what is encompassed within reasonably foreseeable conditions of use.

When driving itself

3.22 The AEVA 2018 states that the insurer is liable for an accident caused by a vehicle 'when driving itself' (Section 2(1)). This will be easily met in Level 5 vehicles without the capability for user control and therefore no transition. For Level 4 vehicles, Section 8 of the AEVA 2018 states that a vehicle is 'driving itself' if it is 'operating in a mode in which it is not being controlled and does not need to be monitored by an individual'. Further, there is some indication that a vehicle in the process of transition will not be classed as driving itself, and therefore claims will be made under the RTA 1988 and not the AEVA 2018.[65] Moreover, indication is that the vehicle user will not be under responsibility to take back control of the vehicle if offered and will be able to decline;[66] transitional liability will therefore rest with the manufacturer and fall under the AEVA 2018. This, however, is not expressly set out within the legislation.

Road or other public place

3.23 The AEVA 2018 covers vehicles on a 'road or other public place' which is identical to the coverage required under the RTA 1988. The term 'road' is defined in the RTA 1988 as 'any highway and any other road to which the public has access'.[67] As noted by Lord Sands in *Harrison v Hill*:[68]

> any road may be regarded as a road to which the public have access upon which members of the public are to be found who have not obtained access either by overcoming a physical obstruction or in defiance of prohibition express or implied.[69]

The EU, through the CJEU's interpretation of the Directives[70] in *Vnuk*,[71] has widened this significantly by stating that a tractor on private land required insurance as long as use of that vehicle was 'consistent with the normal function of that vehicle'.[72] This was slightly reined in by the CJEU in *Rodrigues*[73] who held that 'use' covers 'any use of a vehicle as a means of transport'.[74] The

65 Note the letter from John Hayes MP to the House of Commons Select Committee on the Automated and Electric Vehicles Bill, http://data.parliament.uk/DepositedPapers/files/DEP2017-0688/Letter_to_Committee_-_Contributory_Negligence.pdf, accessed 31 August 2018.
66 Ibid.
67 Section 192(1) RTA 1988.
68 *Harrison v Hill*, 1932 JC 13.
69 Ibid., 17.
70 Sixth Consolidated Motor Insurance Directive (n 28).
71 *Case C-162/13 Vnuk v Zavarovalnica Triglav dd* [2016] RTR 10.
72 Ibid.
73 *Case C-514/16 Rodrigues de Andrade and another v Proença Salvador (ECJ)* [2018] 4 WLR 75.
74 Ibid., [38].

UK Department for Transport has been consulting on the UK's approach to *Vnuk*,[75] particularly in light of the UK's exit from the EU, and results of this consultation are expected soon. Nevertheless, at time of writing autonomous vehicles fall under the Motor Insurance Directives[76] and the UK is within the Directive's remit. This means that autonomous vehicles being tested or used on private land, including agricultural machinery, should be covered by the relevant policy of motor insurance.

The single insurance model

3.24 Instead of the proposed product liability model, the chosen insurance model was based on the 'single insurer', to supplement the insurance provisions of the RTA 1988.[77] The 'single insurer model' was a proposition made by the insurance industry.[78] Consequently, insurance required for the user remains intact, and fault-based liability remains for user fault. However, the vehicle is also required to be insured in the same policy, with both damage caused by the driver and damage caused as a result of the vehicle's technological failure covered (see AEVA 2018 Schedule 1 Paragraph 19 (2)). Once compensation is paid to the third party, the insurer will be able to recover this from the manufacturer under the laws of product liability.

Insurance cover

3.25 The core insurance provision relating to the insurance system within the AEVA 2018 is Section 2(1), which states:

> When (a) an accident is caused by an automated vehicle when driving itself, (b) the vehicle is insured at the time of the accident, and (c) an insured person or any other person suffers damage as a result of the accident, the insurer is liable for that damage.

This provision widens insurer liability beyond conventional vehicle liability to include compensation for all persons within the vehicle where a vehicle's

75 Department for Transport, 'Technical consultation on motor insurance: Consideration of the European Court of Justice ruling in the case of Damijan Vnuk v Zavarovalnica Triglav d.d (C-162/13)' (December 2016), https://assets.publishing.service.gov.uk/government/uploads/system/uploads/attachment_data/file/602216/motor-insurance-vnuk-v-triglav.pdf, accessed 29 August 2018.

76 See Communication from the Commission to the European Parliament, the Council, the European Economic and Social Committee, the Committee of the Regions, 'On the road to automated mobility: An EU strategy for mobility of the future', Brussels, COM (2018), 283 final, 10–11, https://ec.europa.eu/transport/sites/transport/files/3rd-mobility-pack/com20180283_en.pdf, accessed 15 October 2018.

77 'Pathways to Driverless Cars: Government Response (n 7)', [3.11].

78 See Association of British Insurers and Thatcham Research, 'Pathway to Driverless Cars: Proposals to support advanced driver assistance systems and automated vehicle technologies: Response of the Association of British Insurers and Thatcham Research' (June 2016), 10, www.abi.org.uk/globalassets/sitecore/files/documents/consultation-papers/2016/09/090916_abi_thatcham_response_ccav_automated_driving_consultation.pdf, accessed 30 August 2018.

malfunction (technical or otherwise) causes damage. The onus on insuring is on the 'owner' of the vehicle. Further, Section 2(2) is an identical provision to Section 2(1), with the only difference being that where vehicles are legally uninsured, either via Section 144(2) RTA 1988 (Section 2(2)(c)(i) AEVA 2018), or because the vehicle is in the public service of the Crown (Section 2(2)(c)(ii) AEVA 2018), the owner of the vehicle is liable.

Causation

3.26 Section 2(1)[79] contains two elements of causation. First, the accident must be 'caused by' an automated vehicle 'driving itself'. Second, the damage must be suffered 'as a result' of the accident. Whilst, *prima facie*, the wording 'caused by' is similar to that for conventional vehicles,[80] this has greater limitations. The RTA 1988 uses the term 'caused by or arising out of the use of the vehicle' for conventional vehicles, which are two distinct terms. The term 'caused by', which is also contained in the AEVA 2018, connotes a '"direct" or "proximate" relationship of cause and effect'.[81] The term 'arising out of the use of' (not contained in the AEVA 2018) carries a much wider interpretation which 'is less immediate but it still carries a sense of consequence'.[82] For example, in *Dunthorne v Bentley*[83] this was interpreted as involving the deceased who exited the vehicle to wave after her friend in another vehicle, because the victim would not have exited the vehicle had she not run out of petrol. Moreover, in *Holden v UK Insurance*[84] the Court of Appeal held that this could be extended so far as to include the repair of a vehicle in a garage. As noted by the Court in *Wastell v Woodward*,[85] however, this is a case of 'fact and degree',[86] with slightly altered scenarios[87] carrying greater remoteness of damage falling outside of this provision.

3.27 The AEVA 2018 seemingly departs from this by negating the words 'arising out of' and 'use' and including the term 'when driving itself'. It is submitted that the term 'driving itself' is related to the vehicle in motion, rather than a stationary vehicle. *Mcquaid v Anderton*[88] reinforces this in motoring

---

79 And Section 2(2) AEVA 2018.

80 The interpretations of the terms 'caused by' and 'arising out of' (arguably similar to 'as a result of') as noted by Prof Robert Merkin QC and Margaret Hemsworth, *Law of Motor Insurance* (2nd edition, Sweet and Maxwell, 2015), 410, are often interchangeable.

81 As referred to in *UK Insurance Ltd v Holden and another* [2017] EWCA Civ 259, [66].

82 Ibid.

83 [1999] Lloyd's Rep IR 560.

84 *UK Insurance Ltd v R&S Pilling (t/a Phoenix Engineering)* [2017] EWCA Civ 259. Note that by the time this book is published, the Supreme Court will have decided this case.

85 *Christopher Wastell v The Estate of Gordon John Woodward (Deceased), Chaucer Syndicates Limited* 2017 WL 00956511, [19].

86 Ibid., [19].

87 Ibid. As noted by the court in this case involving a person crossing the road after affixing a sign to a burger van: 'if the deceased had been returning across the road to a stall set up separately to his van then the insurers would be off the hook' [19].

88 [1981] 1 WLR 154.

law by finding that the term 'driving' generally connotes, 'a person sitting in the driving seat directing and controlling *the movement of the vehicle* by means of a steering wheel, using the brakes as and when required, the engine being used for propulsion' (emphasis added).[89] This would clearly not cover vehicles being maintained or that are stationary, such as covered in conventional motor insurance;[90] in these circumstances it is likely that the conventional motor insurance part of the policy would be used to the benefit of third-party claimants.

Insurer/owner liability

3.28 Section 2(1) (and Section 2(2) for vehicle owners) AEVA 2018 connotes that payment is made regardless of fault, which is determined later when the insurer recovers from the responsible party.[91]

Damage

3.29 The term 'damage' in this instance is rather narrowly defined. Under Section 2(3), damage excludes:

> (a) the automated vehicle, (b) goods carried for hire or reward in or on that vehicle or in or on any trailer (whether or not coupled) drawn by it, or (c) property in the custody, or under the control, of – (i) the insured person…or (ii) the person in charge of the automated vehicle at the time of the accident (where subsection (2) applies).

This, at least partially, negates the usefulness of the extension of the Act to the user of the vehicle, as the property of the person 'in charge of the vehicle' will not be covered, but puts the law in line with the RTA 1988.[92] The equitability of this is debatable and based on an ownership model conducive of late stages of automation where vehicles could increasingly be owned by business or the State and could increasingly be shared,[93] compared with those who own a vehicle with fewer resources, and with a significantly higher cost of vehicle repair or replacement.[94] Nevertheless, uncertainty is bound to exist in terms of defining 'the person in charge of the vehicle', particularly at Level 5 where there is no driver's seat and therefore limited indication as to who is in charge at that point.

---

89 Ibid.

90 See *UK Insurance Ltd* (n 84) and *Wastell* (n 85).

91 See paras 3.30–3.33.

92 See compulsory cover in Section 144(3) RTA 1988.

93 See, for example, Jeffery B. Greenblatt and Susan Shaheen, 'Automated Vehicles, On-Demand Mobility, and Environmental Impacts' (2015) *Current Sustainable/Renewable Energy Reports*, Vol. 2, No. 3, 74–81. Deloitte, 'The future of mobility: What's next? Tomorrow's mobility ecosystem – and how to succeed in it' (2016, Deloitte University Press), 5, www2.deloitte.com/za/en/pages/consumer-industrial-products/articles/the_future_of_mobility_whats_next.html, accessed 31 August 2018.

94 KPMG, 'Will autonomous vehicles put the brakes on the collision parts business?' (2017), 9–10, www.kpmg-institutes.com/content/dam/kpmg/manufacturing-institute/pdf/2017/collision-parts-whitepaper.pdf, accessed 28 August 2018.

Recovery

Manufacturer

3.30 Under Section 5(1), once the insurer or vehicle owner has settled[95] the victim's claim they are able to recoup the money from 'any other person liable to the injured party in respect of the accident'. If the accident is caused by vehicle defect, then the recovery of damages will be under product liability against the vehicle manufacturer.[96] Of course, it will be required to be proven that the accident was caused when the vehicle was driving itself at the time, which could be a significant challenge.

3.31 Insurers are therefore working to ensure that there is an 'adequate and open access to crash data'[97] from within the vehicle, which will provide evidence as to whether the vehicle was in automated mode.[98] Autonomous vehicles are likely to be fitted with cameras both inside and outside the vehicle and the software will also contain significant data.[99] In proposals for a 'Data Storage System for Automatically Commanded Steering Function' (DSSA), both pre- and post-crash data for Level 3 vehicles and above will be stored.[100] Both the Society for Motor Manufacturers (SMMT) and the Association of British Insurers (ABI) argue that the DSSA should be regulated internationally, most likely by the United Nations Economic Commission for Europe (UNECE) to ensure harmonisation with other jurisdictions.[101] Of course, a clear set of internationally agreed standards in the holding and provision of data to insurers and others is going to be key, albeit contentious, particularly in light of the General Data Protection Regulation 2018 (GDPR).[102] The insurance industry is requesting only certain data to be held in relation to accidents,

95 Defined under Section 5(2), 'the amount of the insurer's or vehicle owner's liability is settled when it is established – (a) by a judgment or decree, (b) by an award in arbitral proceedings or by an arbitration, or (c) by an enforceable agreement'.

96 For detailed discussion on product liability see Chapter 4 of this book.

97 ABI and Thatcham (n 78), 19.

98 See, for example, the evidence provided to the Automated and Electric Vehicles Public Bill Committee by the Association of British Insurers, Senior Policy Advisor: 'insurers are clear that we only want the data when a collision has occurred to confirm whether the car was in automated mode or not' (Public Bill Committee, *Automated and Electric Vehicles Bill* (Tuesday 31 October 2017 (morning) first sitting), 6). It was noted later that a distinction could be drawn 'between the data that insurers need to make this Bill operational and the data from cars that would be useful to understand claims', 11.

99 Phillipe Baecke and Lorenzo Bocca, 'The value of vehicle telematics data in insurance risk selection processes' (2017) *Decision Support Systems and Electric Commerce*, Vol. 98, 69–79, 69. The authors note that there will be a 'massive flow of data' resulting from the internet of things.

100 The ABI argue for 'Standardised non-discriminating access to this data for all parties with a legitimate Interest in an individual case'. See ABI and Thatcham (n 78), 19.

101 See ibid. and Society for Motor Manufacturers and Traders, 'Connected and Autonomous Vehicles: Position Paper' (February 2017), 12, www.smmt.co.uk/wp-content/uploads/sites/2/SMMT-CAV-position-paper-final.pdf, accessed 31 August 2018.

102 This will be discussed in the Cyber Security Chapter. Regulation (EU) 2016/679 of the European Parliament and of the Council of 27 April 2016 on the protection of natural persons with regard to the processing of personal data and on the free movement of such data, and repealing Directive 95/46/EC (General Data Protection Regulation) (2016) OJ L 119.

which relates to whether the vehicle was in automated mode, with access in a timely fashion to ensure that it remains relevant.[103]

3.32 In relation to claims against manufacturers under the AEVA 2018, there is potential for the manufacturer to use defences in cases of recovery, which would mean the insurer would be required to cover the cost of the claim.[104] As noted in the government's response, however, whilst there may be cases in which liability is disputed, both manufacturers and insurers are likely to develop processes over time to ensure quicker recovery.[105]

3.33 There is further a clear balance to be met here in claiming damages against manufacturers. Numerous claims against manufacturers could be detrimental for technological development, with an overexposure for manufacturers leading to a 'chilling effect' on innovation.[106] However, this may also have a positive impact on the safety of the technology, encouraging manufacturers to take extra care to ensure that their vehicles are safe for public use – the 'defensive design' of technology'.[107]

Failure to update software, recovery and exclusions

3.34 The AEVA 2018 has two provisions relating to failure to update software or prohibited software alterations. The first, under Section 4(1), allows the insurer to contractually exclude or limit its liability suffered by the insured person. It is submitted that this would likely be through an exclusion clause. Second, under Section 4(4), the insurer is able to recover damages paid to victims from an individual who is not insured under the policy in question. The amount recoverable is determined by the insurance policy. Both Section 4(1) and 4(4) are identical in relation to the subject matter, although Section 4(1) is written in the present tense by using the term 'occurring' whereas Section 4(4) is written in the past tense utilising the term 'occurred'. Due to the identical nature of the core provisions contained within both sections, it is important to quote only Section 4(1), which states:

---

103 As noted by David Williams, Chair of the Automated Driving Insurer Group in evidence provided to the Automated and Electric Bills Committee, 'there is no point us getting the data three months later'. See Public Bills Committee, *Automated and Electric Vehicles Bill* (Tuesday 31 October 2017 (morning) first sitting), 12.

104 'Pathway to driverless cars: Government Response' (n 7), [3.15]. The government response here did not mention recovery by the vehicle owner against the manufacturer, although it is likely that the manufacturer can use defences against the owner, meaning the owner covering the cost of the claim.

105 Ibid., [3.14]. Again, this is likely to apply in relation to claims between vehicle owner and manufacturer despite not being mentioned in the government response.

106 Schellekens (n 60), [4.2.2].

107 Ibid. See Richard M. Morrow, 'Technology Issues and Product Liability' in Janet R. Hunziker and Trevor O. Jones (eds), *Product Liability and Innovation: Managing Risk in an Uncertain Environment* (National Academy Press, 1994), 27: 'This practice of "defensive design" incorporates a rigorous and careful application of engineering methods. It includes formal engineering analysis, testing, and anticipating problems through fault-mode and worst-case analysis methods.'

An insurance policy in respect of an automated vehicle may exclude or limit the insurer's liability under section 2(1) for damage suffered by an insured person arising from an accident occurring as a direct result of –

(a) Software alterations made by an insured person, or with an insured person's knowledge, that were prohibited under the policy, or
(b) a failure to install safety-critical software updates that an insured person knew, or ought reasonably to have known, were safety-critical.[108]

3.35 The requirement that the accident occurred 'as a direct result' of the 'software alterations' (or 'failure to install safety critical software updates'), will be difficult to establish, particularly if there are a number of potential causes of the accident. Furthermore, there are a number of key terms which require defining within this provision and other complexities associated with it. 'Safety-critical' involves particular complexity. Lord Craig noted in the House of Lords that the term is 'meant to sound reassuring' until it is asked 'how "safety-critical" is defined and who decides'.[109] Whilst the Act makes no mention of the decision as to whether an update is 'safety-critical', there is some further clarification in Section 4(6)(b), which states that 'software updates are "safety-critical" if it would be unsafe to use the vehicle in question without the updates being installed'. The term 'unsafe' here is undefined, although a potential comparator could be in the definition of the term 'unsafe' in conventional motor insurance.[110]

3.36 Merkin and Hemsworth note that 'unsafe' in conventional motor insurance law tends to point towards mechanical defects such as those affecting brakes and tyres,[111] although this does not extend to a vehicle driving at excessive speed[112] (which is due to the user of the vehicle, rather than a defect emanating from the vehicle). However, where the speed of the vehicle or lighting defects are caused by the user failing to update software or tampering with the software, this author submits that, this would likely fall within this provision. This is because in conventional motor vehicles the speed of the vehicle is not based around the vehicle itself, but rather the user's actions in the vehicle, whereas speed in the autonomous vehicle when in automated mode would be specifically based on the software. However, this author submits that this could lead to the bizarre conclusion that the vehicle is deemed roadworthy when being driven at an unsafe speed by the user, but suddenly becomes unsafe when in automated mode.

108 Section 4(4) AEVA 2018.

109 Lord Craig of Radley (CB) Automated and Electric Vehicles Bill (2nd Reading), 20 February 2018, Column 25.

110 *Barrett v London General Insurance Company, Limited* [1935] 1 KB 238, 241. See Professor Robert Merkin QC and Margaret Hemsworth (n 80), 219.

111 Professor Robert Merkin QC and Margaret Hemsworth (n 80), 219.

112 Ibid.

3.37 Another term in Section 4(4) which is not defined in the Act but was previously used in conventional motor insurance law is 'ought reasonably to know'. For example, the MIB Uninsured Drivers' Agreement 1999 uses a similar term by excluding compensation to a passenger who enters a vehicle where they 'know or ought to have known' the vehicle was stolen.[113] The House of Lords in *White v White*[114] interpreted the term as meaning that the passenger had either 'actual' knowledge or 'blind eye' knowledge. This would include 'a passenger (who) had information from which he drew the conclusion that the driver might well not be insured',[115] and it 'is apt to include knowledge which an honest person who enters the vehicle voluntarily would have…and "refrains from asking questions"'.[116] However, as noted by his lordship, 'it is not apt to include mere carelessness or negligence'.[117] This is therefore a slightly narrower definition due to the need to ensure the provision's compatibility with EU law.[118]

3.38 Applying this interpretation to autonomous vehicles, the failure to make obvious enquiries as to the safety-critical nature of software – despite having the information from which the conclusion could be drawn (such as a user manual), where a reasonable person would have held the updates to be safety-critical – would, it is submitted, fall within this provision. The autonomous vehicle interpretation, however, has the additional challenge in relation to its context. Whereas in conventional motor insurance, 'ought to have known' precedes a clear subject – that is, that the vehicle is stolen – it is submitted that 'ought to reasonably know' in the AEVA 2018 precedes an uncertain subject, a 'safety-critical' update. Consequently, the question arises as to whether, due to the absence of clarity in this term, anyone would have the ability to know the exact safety implications of a software update. Moreover, if an objective test is used to determine knowledge, the question would be the standard of knowledge to impose within this. In tort law, the well-known case of *Nettleship v Weston*[119] provides that a learner driver must have the same standard of care as a competent driver. The rationale behind this is that 'if the driver were to be excused according to the knowledge of the passenger, it would result in endless confusion and injustice'.[120] The author submits that, if this was a similar position for autonomous vehicles, then a high standard of care, even for those with limited technological knowledge, would be needed. This, however, raises further issues in relation to those who may not comprehend the significance of a software update through disability or age. One of the benefits often cited around the introduction of autonomous

113 MIB Uninsured Drivers Agreement 1999, Section 6(1)(e).
114 *White v White and another* [2001] UKHL/9.
115 Ibid., [16].
116 Ibid., [23].
117 Ibid.
118 *Akers and Others v Motor Insurers' Bureau and Another* [2003] EWCA Civ 18, [6].
119 [1971] 2 QB 691.
120 Ibid., 700.

vehicles is the increase of mobility for those with disabilities and both older and younger people.[121] Of course, it is possible that in many circumstances vehicles will be used rather than owned,[122] putting the burden of updating the software on the owner who will be insured. Nevertheless, in cases of autonomous vehicles used and owned by a person with disabilities, it is submitted that an unjustly high burden is placed through this provision, without providing adjustment based on the characteristics of the insured person. This provision is therefore inadequate and should be adjusted, taking into account the individual's characteristics.

3.39 Importantly, as noted by Baroness Sugg CBE, 'the overwhelming majority' of updates will be completed remotely.[123] Nevertheless, it is submitted that further legal challenges are inevitable as the current legislative provisions in the AEVA 2018 on critical software updates are too vague and drawn against the user of the vehicle, regardless of characteristics.[124]

Exclusions and recovery limitations

Exclusions

3.40 Under Section 2(6) AEVA 2018, apart from in relation to software alterations, insurers are unable to limit or exclude liability in any way against either the injured driver or third parties either through contractual or any other exclusions. This provision is clearly different from provisions for conventional vehicles through Sections 148 and 151 RTA 1988. Section 148 lists certain exclusion clauses which cannot be used against a third party, meaning that other exclusion clauses can be utilised.[125] Section 152(2)(a) allows an insurer to repudiate liability for non-disclosure of a material fact. In these cases, the MIB will then step in as an insurer of last resort to compensate victims,

---

121 Society of Motor Manufacturers, 'Connected and Autonomous Vehicles: Revolutionising Mobility in Society' (SMMT International Automotive Summit), 21, www.smmt.co.uk/wp-content/uploads/sites/2/Connected-and-Autonomous-Vehicles-Revolutionising-Mobility-in-Society.pdf, accessed 31 August 2018. Also Deloitte, 'The future of mobility: What's next? Tomorrow's mobility ecosystem – and how to succeed in it' (2016, Deloitte University Press), 5, www2.deloitte.com/za/en/pages/consumer-industrial-products/articles/the_future_of_mobility_whats_next.html, accessed 31 August 2018.

122 Ibid. (Deloitte), 5.

123 Letter from Baroness Sugg CBE to the House of Lords Automated and Electric Vehicles Bill Committee, http://data.parliament.uk/DepositedPapers/files/DEP2018-0391/Baroness_Sugg_letter_-_terminology_in_the_AEV_Bill.pdf, accessed 29 August 2018.

124 It must be remembered that under the Equality Act 2010, age (Section 5) and disability are protected characteristics. With regard to disability, see Section 20(3) in relation to the requirement to make adjustments.

125 Section 148 RTA 1988 (2)(a) the age or physical or mental condition of persons driving the vehicle, (b) the condition of the vehicle, (c) the number of persons that the vehicle carries, (d) the weight or physical characteristics of the goods that the vehicle carries, (e) the time at which or the areas within which the vehicle is used, (f) the horsepower or cylinder capacity or value of the vehicle, (g) the carrying on the vehicle of any particular apparatus, or (h) the carrying on the vehicle of any particular means of identification other than any means of identification required to be carried by or under the Vehicle Excise and Registration Act 1994.

with the MIB requiring the insurer to act as an agent, but paying under the MIB Agreement rather than an insurance policy.[126] This, therefore, has the potential to delay payment of claims as it will need to be determined who was in control of the vehicle to decide whether it is the insurance policy or the MIB Agreements under which the damages will be paid to the third party. This would likely only be investigated by the insurer where they have a valid defence under MIB Agreements, which would provide them with an incentive to delay payment of compensation.

3.41 It is further important to note the absence of a clause relating to stolen vehicles in the AEVA 2018. This is a clause permitted for conventional vehicles under Section 151(2)(b) of the RTA 1988 in relation to third parties, with a person allowing themselves to be carried in or upon a vehicle when they 'knew or had reason to believe the vehicle was stolen or unlawfully taken'[127] being excluded from compensation. This is the only clause permitted under EU law.[128] Whilst this defence is not catered for in legislation, there is potential for a claim to be denied under the tort law defence of *ex turpi causa* (illegality), the premise being that a party cannot benefit from their own criminal act.[129] Due to the recent reframing of the defence in *Patel v Mirza,*[130] it is uncertain as to exactly how this defence would be applied. It must be remembered that under conventional motor insurance the user of the vehicle is a first party and therefore would not be compensated for vehicle theft. However, in relation to a vehicle 'driving itself', the user becomes a passenger for the purposes of insurance. Third parties could debatably claim for damages in stolen vehicle cases; the key discussion pre-*Patel* has been around causation: the accident must have been caused by criminal act.[131] A wider interpretation has

---

126 The MIB requires the insurer to compensate victims as an agent of the MIB but under the MIB Agreements.

127 Section 151(4) RTA 1988.

128 Note that under EU law, Article 13(2) of the Sixth Consolidated Directive (n 28), it is 'vehicles stolen or obtained by violence'. Also within the same provision, Member States may specify that the compensation body is required to compensate. Although note Article 10 (2) which states 'Member States may, however, exclude the payment of compensation by that body in respect of persons who voluntarily entered the vehicle which caused the damage or injury when the body can prove that they knew it was uninsured'. Note there is a significant debate about whether the EU permits exclusion clauses. An exclusion clause for stolen vehicles is permitted under Article 13(1) of the Sixth Consolidated Motor Insurance Directive (n 28). Recent CJEU jurisprudence suggests that 'derogations from the first subparagraph of art. 2(1) of the Second Directive may be made only in that single, specific case', C-287/16 *Fidelidade-Companhia de Seguros SA v Caisse Suisse de Compensation* [2017] RTR 26, [26].

129 This was founded in the case *of Holman v Johnson* (1775) 1 Cowp 341, 343, by Lord Mansfield who stated: 'The principle of public policy is this; *ex dolo malo non oritur actio*. No court will lend its aid to a man who founds his cause of action upon an immoral or an illegal act.'

130 The test for *ex turpi causa* is '(a) considering the underlying purpose of the prohibition which has been transgressed, (b) considering conversely any other relevant public policies which may be rendered ineffective or less effective by denial of the claim, and (c) keeping in mind the possibility of overkill unless the law is applied with a due sense of proportionality'; *Patel v Mirza* [2016] UKSC 42, [101].

131 See *Delaney v Pickett* [2011] EWCA Civ 1532, [37].

been given to this, however, as noted in *Joyce v O'Brien*[132] and later repeated in *Smith v McCracken*[133] in relation to a stolen motor cycle:

> where the character of the joint criminal enterprise is such that it is foreseeable that… parties may be subject to…increased risks of harm as a consequence of the activities…the injury can properly be said to be caused by the criminal act of the claimant even if it results from the negligent or intentional act of another party to the illegal enterprise.[134]

Whilst this may be applicable to a conventional vehicle, its application for autonomous vehicles is more complex. The question arises as to whether vehicle theft in automated mode would lead to a greater risk of harm.

Limitations of recovery

3.42 The extension of compulsory insurance to ensure that users are compensated when the vehicle is in automated mode is limited to one instance. As noted in Section 3(2) AEVA 2018:

> The insurer or owner of an automated vehicle is not liable under section 2 to the person in charge of the vehicle where the accident that it caused was wholly due to the person's negligence in allowing the vehicle to begin driving itself when it was not appropriate to do so.

3.43 This term, it is submitted, is undoubtedly open to interpretation due to the requirement for the accident to be caused 'wholly due to the person's negligence'. The term 'wholly' is likely to impose a significant burden upon the insurer to ensure that there were no other causes of the accident or contributing factors, however minor. For example, if, say A puts his car into automated mode too early, the vehicle is not designed to drive itself on ice and skids to avoid a pedestrian due to non-optimum tyre condition, could this be said to be 'wholly' due to the person's negligence in allowing the vehicle to drive itself? It is submitted that this is unlikely. Sir Oliver Letwin in the House of Commons Committee was critical of the use of the term 'wholly', noting that this provision would be an 'almost impossible thing to establish'[135] and further that the use of the term was 'a very odd thing to do'.[136]

3.44 Finally, the requirement of 'negligence' is a lower standard compared with intentionality or recklessness and the test regarding software updates in Section 4.[137] Inappropriateness in this context is also not defined and will require later interpretation.

132 *Joyce v O'Brien* [2014] 1 WLR 70, [47].

133 [2015] PIQR P19.

134 *Joyce* (n 133).

135 Public Bill Committee, *Automated and Electric Vehicles Bill* (Thursday 2 November (Morning) third sitting), 84 [Sir Oliver Letwin].

136 Ibid., 114.

137 Remember the discussion above on *White v White* in terms of actual or 'blind eye' knowledge; Lord Nicholls distinguishes this from 'negligence or recklessness'.

Uninsured and untraced drivers

3.45 A significant issue which the Act has not resolved concerns the compensation of victims as a result of an accident caused by an uninsured or untraced vehicle. Under conventional motor insurance law, this is the role of the Motor Insurers' Bureau, a body currently funded by the insurance industry.[138] The relationship between the MIB and its members is set out in the MIB's Articles of Association.[139] Furthermore, the MIB's role for conventional vehicles is obligated through the EU Directives[140] as the UK's guarantee fund.

3.46 Notably, the AEVA 2018 does not provide information as to the MIB's responsibility for uninsured or untraced vehicles. The MIB's role is not set out in the RTA 1988 for conventional vehicles either,[141] but rather set out in an Agreement between the MIB and Secretary of State for Transport,[142] which has not, as of yet, been updated to include autonomous vehicles. Nevertheless, it is submitted that it is likely that the MIB will continue to have a role in relation to autonomous vehicles as the fund of last resort and this, it seems, is supported by the insurance industry.

3.47 Questions will undoubtedly arise concerning the interaction between the MIB and manufacturers in relation to accidents caused by a vehicle 'driving itself', but which is not insured. It is submitted that manufacturers should be compensating in these situations rather than the MIB, because manufacturer fault may nevertheless be determined. However, where the vehicle is only partially insured – that is, it is insured only in relation to its conventional use – questions may concern whether the vehicle insurer or manufacturer will be obliged to pay in this instance. The current situation puts the insurer in the position to compensate due to Article 75(2)(a)(1)(iii) of the MIB's Articles of Association, with no obligation upon the manufacturer as it currently stands within the Articles.[143]

3.48 The MIB's role in relation to untraced vehicles is also yet to be determined. Due to the number of cameras and sensors on autonomous vehicles, it is submitted that autonomous vehicles are likely to be easier to trace. Nevertheless, in the case of an unidentified vehicle accident, it is submitted that questions are likely to concern whether the vehicle was conventional or autonomous, as well as, indeed, whether the vehicle was 'driving itself' at the

138 It is compulsory for an insurer undertaking motor insurance in the UK to become a member of the MIB and to contribute to its funding.

139 MIB Articles of Association (n 22).

140 Sixth Consolidated Directive (n 28), Article 10.

141 Although note that the RTA 1988 does contain a provision relating the requirement for a policy 'to be issued by authorised insurer' (Section 145(2)). An 'authorised insurer' is defined in Section 95(2) RTA 1988 as 'an insurer who is a member of the Motor Insurers Bureau (a company limited by guarantee and incorporated under the Companies Act 1929 on 14th June 1946)'.

142 MIB Uninsured Drivers Agreement 2015, www.mib.org.uk/media/166917/2015-uninsured-drivers-agreement-england-scotland-wales.pdf, accessed 30 August 2018.

143 Although there is nothing to prevent the manufacturer from being sued by the victim under product liability through the Consumer Protection Act 1987.

time. However, questions are undoubtedly going to arise as to whether the MIB should get funding from manufacturers also to cater for the potential for accidents caused by untraced autonomous vehicles.

3.49 The AEVA 2018, it seems, limits the role of Article 75 of the MIB's Articles of Association compared with conventional motor insurance in relation to the use of exclusions. Under compulsory motor insurance law, an insurer can deny payment to a third party under its insurance policy if an exclusion clause is breached by the assured.[144] Liability would then transfer to the MIB who require insurers to act as agents and compensate victims, but under the MIB Uninsured Drivers' Agreement rather than the insurance policy.[145] With Section 2(6) AEVA 2018 prohibiting virtually all exclusions, the requirement of this process becomes redundant, apart from potentially where an exclusion is used in relation to software updates (Section 4(1) AEVA 2018). The question arises as to whether the MIB will step in to ensure compensation of the insured person where the software update exclusion has been breached, which is currently not provided for in the AEVA 2018 or MIB Agreements.

144 See *Bristol Alliance v Williams* (n 16).
145 Article 75 of the MIB Article of Association (n 22).

CHAPTER 4

Product liability

Lucy McCormick

Introduction

4.1 One of the key unknowns in relation to autonomous vehicles is how the courts will approach the issue of liability if one is involved in a collision. As the technology becomes more advanced, there are more potential parties to a claim, including the driver, the vehicle manufacturer, the software supplier and so on.

4.2 At present, there is no specific legislation in England and Wales governing the ultimate liability for accidents caused by autonomous vehicles.[1] Nor has there been any litigation in relation to this in the courts of England and Wales.

4.3 Nonetheless, it is possible to make some observations on the likely liability position:

(a) As the technology stands at present, the driver of a Level 2[2] vehicle is still highly likely to be found liable for any collision caused by their vehicle's behaviour. This is because the expectation remains that the driver will be alert and monitoring the vehicle at all times. However, if the collision was contributed to by a failure of ADAS,[3] then there would be the scope for the driver to bring, in turn, a claim against the manufacturer – probably under the Consumer Protection Act 1987, but also potentially in negligence or breach of contract. The manufacturer might then be able to sue any third-party software or component supplier for breach of contract.

(b) In respect of more advanced vehicles available in the future, in most circumstances liability for a collision caused by a commercially available Level 4/5 vehicle would rest with the manufacturer, on the basis that in such a vehicle it would be reasonable for an occupant to disengage entirely from the driving task. Indeed, a Level 4/5 vehicle might not

1 Although there is legislation in relation to the mandatory insurance of autonomous vehicles – see Chapter 3.

2 For the various 'levels' of autonomous vehicles, see Chapter 1 and the SAE J3016 standard.

3 Advanced driver assistance systems – such as automatic emergency braking or 'lane keep assist'.

even have a steering wheel. Again, the manufacturer could well have a claim in turn against a third-party software or component supplier.

(c) The real uncertainty concerns the position if and when Level 3 vehicles are made commercially available. Society, and the courts, will need to reach a view as to what extent it is reasonable to expect the driver to monitor the vehicle when it is in 'self-driving' mode, and as to how quickly one can expect a driver to retake control in an emergency. There are real practical concerns about both of these points, given that several tests have found that occupants of autonomous vehicles struggle to maintain situational awareness for any length of time, and can take in the region of 25 seconds to retake control of a vehicle once distracted.[4]

4.4 In practice, the key legislation in relation to liability for autonomous vehicles is currently the Consumer Protection Act 1987 (CPA 1987). It is also possible that claims could be brought for negligence or breach of contract.

Product liability under the CPA 1987

Introduction to the CPA 1987

4.5 The CPA 1987 implements European Council Directive 85/374/EEC (the Product Liability Directive) and is to be construed in accordance with the provisions of that Directive. It created a form of 'strict liability' where a product is shown to be defective.

4.6 The Product Liability Directive was intended to ensure a fair apportionment of risk between the consumer and the producer, with a view to balancing the need to protect consumers with the desire to allow space for producers to develop innovative products. The burden of proof is on the claimant to prove that the product was defective, and that the defect caused damage. Once that is done, there is strict liability, subject to certain statutory defences.

4.7 The Product Liability Directive and the CPA 1987 both came into force before autonomous vehicles were a realistic prospect. Therefore, it is not surprising that the legislation is in certain respects a poor fit in relation to such technology. Notably:

(a) There is no provision for liability for damage to the defective product itself, which is obviously problematic in an automotive context where vehicles may cost many thousands of pounds.[5]

(b) There is no provision for liability for damage to property which is not ordinarily intended for private use, or is not intended by the person

4 K. Naughton, 'Ford's Dozing Engineers Side With Google in Full Autonomy Push', Bloomberg (17 February 2017), www.bloomberg.com/news/articles/2017-02-17/ford-s-dozing-engineers-side-with-google-in-full-autonomy-push, accessed 27 August 2018; Alexander Eriksson and Neville A. Stanton, 'Takeover Time in Highly Automated Vehicles' (2017) HUMAN FACTORS Vol. 59, No. 4, 689–705, www.journals.sagepub.com/doi/abs/10.1177/0018720816685832, accessed 27 August 2018.

5 Section 5(2).

suffering the loss mainly for his own private use.[6] In practice, this means that claims for property damage can only be brought by consumers. Given that many vehicles are used in a primarily commercial context, this removes substantial swathes of potential claims from the ambit of the CPA 1987.[7]

(c) The CPA 1987 provides for a ten-year 'long stop' provision, which means that a claim can only be made in the first ten years of a product's lifespan. This limits its utility in the context of vehicles which may be used for much longer.[8]

What is a product?

4.8 The CPA 1987 provides that a product means 'any goods or electricity and … includes a product which is comprised in another product, whether by virtue of being a component part or raw material or otherwise'.[9]

4.9 This definition clearly encompasses the supply of a complete autonomous vehicle. It would also include any tangible component of that vehicle.

4.10 However, when considering the constituent parts of an autonomous vehicle, one important aspect is the software. There is a debate as to whether software is capable of amounting to a 'product' within the CPA 1987. There is presently no case directly on point in a CPA 1987 context. It is tolerably clear that software supplied on a tangible medium such as a disk would be considered a product.[10] However, there is a question mark over the status of software supplied via a non-tangible medium – that is to say via the internet or over a telecommunications system. By analogy, it is highly likely that software pre-loaded on to the on-board computer of a vehicle would be considered a product and thus come within the CPA 1987. However, an 'over the air' update to an autonomous vehicle (such as those utilised by Tesla) would fall into a grey area.

4.11 There is some useful case law touching upon this issue – albeit in a non-CPA 1987 context. In *St Albans DC v International Computers Ltd*,[11] the Court of Appeal expressed the view that software was not 'goods' for the purpose of the Sale of Goods Act 1979, but distinguished the situation where

6 Section 5(3).

7 Although claims for death or personal injury may still be brought under the CPA 1987 by non-consumers.

8 According to the SMMT 2018 Automotive Sustainability Report, 'The average age of a car at scrappage in 2015 reached 13.9 years, which is on a par with the 2014 performance. The lowest scrappage age, 13 years, was recorded in 2009, a result of government's scrappage scheme. Furthermore, the average age of a vehicle on the road has increased, from 6.8 years in 2003 to 7.8 recorded in 2015', www.smmt.co.uk/industry-topics/sustainability/average-vehicle-age, accessed 27 August 2018.

9 Section 1(2).

10 See *St Albans City & District Council v International Computers Ltd* [1996] 4 All ER 481, 493.

11 [1996] 4 All ER 481.

the software was supplied on disk. The same distinction was applied in the context of an electronic database in *Your Response Ltd v Datateam Business Media Ltd.*[12] More recently, in *Computer Associates UK Ltd v The Software Incubator Ltd,*[13] the Court of Appeal has held that the supply of software in the form of a download is not a 'sale of goods' for the purposes of the Commercial Agents (Council Directive) Regulations 1993. Gloster LJ (with whom both Henderson LJ and Irwin LJ agreed) expressed sympathy for the argument that the distinction between software supplied on a tangible medium and software downloaded from the internet is outdated.[14] She noted that the distinction leads to odd and inconsistent results – for example, where software was initially downloaded, but a backup copy was subsequently provided on disk, the backup supply would be a supply of goods but the initial supply would not.[15] However, Gloster LJ concluded that it was not for the court to depart from the weight of prevailing authority by giving 'goods' a sufficiently wide interpretation to cover software supplied in electronic form.[16] She took the view that this was an area where reform needed to come from the legislature and not via judicial interpretation.[17]

4.12 On balance, at present it is more likely than not that the courts would apply the *Computer Associates* approach in a product liability context, and thus consider 'pure' software to be outside the ambit of the CPA 1987. There may therefore be some tactical advantage to programmers in supplying updates 'over the air', rather than by supplying them on a USB flash drive to be physically inserted into a vehicle's on-board computer.

What is a defect?

4.13 The CPA 1987 defines 'defect' at Section 3(1):

> if the safety of the product is not such as persons generally are entitled to expect; and for those purposes 'safety', in relation to a product, shall include safety with respect to products comprised in that product and safety in the context of risks of damage to property, as well as in the context of risks of death or personal injury.

4.14 At Section 3(2), the CPA 1987 provides guidelines as to what 'persons generally are entitled to expect', indicating that:

---

12 [2015] EWCA Civ 281.

13 [2018] EWCA Civ 518.

14 For example, at [50].

15 At [51]. Similar criticisms were made by Lord Penrose in the Outer House of the Court of Session in *Beta Computers (Europe) Ltd v Adobe Systems (Europe) Ltd* [1996] SLT 604, commenting at 608 that such reasoning 'appears to emphasise the role of the physical medium, and to relate the transaction in the medium to sale or hire of goods. It would have the somewhat odd result that the dominant characteristic of the complex product, in terms of value or of the significant interests of parties, would be subordinated to the medium by which it was transmitted to the user in analysing the true nature and effect of the contract.'

16 At [55].

17 At [67].

(2) In determining for the purposes of subsection (1) above what persons generally are entitled to expect in relation to a product all the circumstances shall be taken into account, including—

(a) the manner in which, and purposes for which, the product has been marketed, its get-up, the use of any mark in relation to the product and any instructions for, or warnings with respect to, doing or refraining from doing anything with or in relation to the product;
(b) what might reasonably be expected to be done with or in relation to the product; and
(c) time when the product was supplied by its producer to another; and nothing in this section shall require a defect to be inferred from the fact alone that the safety of a product which is supplied after that time is greater than the safety of the product in question.

4.15 Guidance on how to interpret what 'persons generally are entitled to expect' has been given in several cases, notably *A v National Blood Authority*[18] and *Wilkes v DePuy International Limited.*[19] In *A v NBA*, Burton J held that the relevant question was what the public's 'legitimate expectation' was (rather than what the public in fact expected). However, in *Wilkes*, Hickinbottom J commented that he found that Burton J's use of the phrase 'legitimate expectation' was 'an unnecessary and unhelpful gloss' on the CPA 1987.[20] He stated that the level of safety is 'not to be assessed by reference to actual expectations of an actual or even a notional individual or group of individuals', and made it clear that the test was an objective one.[21] He concluded that

> in considering whether a product suffered from a defect, the court must assess the appropriate level of safety, exercising its judgment, and taking into account the information and the circumstances before it, whether or not an actual or notional patient or patients…would in fact have considered each of those factors and all of that information.[22]

The dicta of Hickinbottom J is likely to be helpful for producers of autonomous vehicles, given that the actual expectations of customers in relation to the capabilities of such technologies may be unrealistic.

4.16 Guidance on what 'circumstances' might be relevant was provided in *Wilkes*, where Hickinbottom J indicated that assessment of whether a product is defective requires a 'holistic approach…involving the application of judgment to the exercise of balancing all relevant considerations'.[23] He noted that the question of which circumstances are relevant and the weight to be given to each are 'quintessentially dependent upon the particular facts of any case'.

4.17 Notably, the definition of defective under the CPA 1987 includes at Section 3(2)(a) consideration of 'any instructions for, or warnings with

18 [2001] 3 All ER 289.
19 [2016] EWHC 3096.
20 Ibid., [71].
21 Ibid., [69].
22 Ibid., [72].
23 Ibid., [78].

respect to, doing or refraining from doing anything with or in relation to the product'. It follows that instructions and warnings should be considered when assessing defectiveness. Good instructions and warnings can render products with potential dangers safe, whilst poor instructions and inadequate warnings can be reasons to find a product unsafe. Manufacturers have a duty to warn of hidden dangers and how to safely use a product. Normally, in an automotive context this is done simply through warnings in the user's manual. However, in the context of highly automated cars more obvious warnings may be necessary, or even driver training at point of sale. This is particularly so in relation to Level 3 vehicles where in practice the vehicle can take over the driving task for an extended period but the driver is nonetheless supposed to monitor the vehicle throughout – drivers may mistakenly believe that there is no need to continue monitoring the vehicle. Different manufacturers are devising different strategies in relation to this. In Tesla vehicles, for example, warnings are provided at multiple levels, including in the owner's manual, in the release notes for new software releases, in a user agreement required before enabling autopilot for the first time or after an ignition cycle that concluded with autopilot being switched off, and in a dialogue box that appears every time autopilot is activated reminding the driver to always keep their hands on the wheel and to be prepared to take over at any time. Tesla supplements this by actively monitoring driver engagement, activating an escalating series of warnings if the driver's hands are not detected on the steering wheel.[24] In contrast, General Motors is developing a 'Super Cruise' system which is intended to use facial recognition systems to ensure the driver is keeping an eye on the road even when the system is engaged. Such systems will offer potential arguments against an allegation of 'failure to warn' users of the need to pay continual attention to the road.

4.18 It is important to note that the CPA 1987 does not restrict consideration to the uses specified by the producer. As long as what is done can reasonably be expected, liability can arise. Therefore, there may be liability for some misuses of the product as long as these were foreseeable and not unreasonable.

---

24 At time of writing, there were reports that consumers had begun to circumvent this by wedging a whole orange into the spokes of the steering wheel, the pressure of which (in combination with the micro-movements of the car itself travelling along the road) could 'fool' Tesla's software into thinking that the driver's hands were on the wheel. It has also been reported that third-party sellers are marketing accessories deliberately designed to 'fool' Tesla's software, enabling the occupant of the car to 'drive' completely hands-free. The US National Highway Traffic Safety Administration (NHTSA) issued a cease and desist order in relation to one such seller in June 2018 – see www.theverge.com/2018/6/19/17479316/tesla-autopilot-buddy-aftermarket-nhtsa, accessed 27 August 2018. The latter gives rise to a potentially interesting liability situation. In a German case, a manufacturer of a motorcycle was found liable in negligence for failing to supervise the accessories market when parts made by another producer, but aimed at his products, rendered them dangerous: (1986) NJW 1009. In principle it is possible that the use of accessories with a product would be something 'done in relation to the product' and thus be a ground for potentially treating the product as defective.

In an Austrian Supreme Court case in 1998, the court imposed liability on the producer of cycle handlebars because they had not warned they were unsuitable for racing conditions.[25] Although not explicitly advertised for use in extreme conditions, the producer was held to be liable because it had been informed that leading Austrian sportsmen were using their products in cycle races. This may be relevant to autonomous vehicles if manufacturers become aware – for example, from YouTube videos – that consumers are misusing their products. Drawing the line as to which misuses are considered foreseeable will inevitably be difficult in practice.

4.19 Interestingly, a product which is inherently unsafe is not necessarily defective. See, for example, *B v McDonald's Restaurants Ltd*,[26] where scalding hot coffee in suitably substantial polystyrene cups was not considered to be defective. In *Wilkes*,[27] Hickinbottom J noted that no effective medicinal product can be entirely safe, and concluded[28] that safety was 'inherently and necessarily a relative concept' and that 'the potential benefits (including potential utility) of such a product has to be balanced against the risks'. In doing this, Hickinbottom J again moved away from Burton J in *A v NBA*,[29] who had appeared to suggest that a risk–benefit analysis was not relevant to the CPA 1987. This potentially opens a path for an argument in an appropriate case that the overall safety and societal benefits offered by autonomous vehicles[30] should play a part in the assessment of the court.

4.20 It is for the claimant to establish that the product was defective, on the balance of probability. However, the Court of Appeal in *Ide v ATB Sales Ltd*[31] held that under the CPA 1987 it is unnecessary for the judge to ascertain the precise cause of the defect. This is certainly useful in an autonomous vehicle context, where the piece of code which prompted a particular collision may not be discernible even to the original programmers of the vehicle, given the frequent use of 'machine learning' in this context.[32]

4.21 As well as establishing a defect, the claimant must also establish that the defect caused the loss claimed.

Who can be sued under the CPA 1987?

4.22 This is dealt with in Section 2 of the CPA 1987. Under Section 2(2), three categories of person are inherently liable, namely:

25 Decision of 28 April 1998, 10 Ob 399/97t: see *Hayböck* [1998] 6 Consum LJ 518–519.
26 [2002] EWHC 490 (QB).
27 *Wilkes* (n 19).
28 Ibid., [65].
29 *A v NBA* (n 18).
30 E.g. in mobilizing partially sighted and elderly citizens.
31 [2008] EWCA Civ 424.
32 Machine learning is an application of artificial intelligence that provides systems with the ability to automatically learn and improve from experience without being explicitly programmed.

(a) producers, being the manufacturers of the product;[33]
(b) those putting their name on a product or using a trade mark or other distinguishing mark and holding themselves out as the producer of the product (often known as 'own branders');
(c) the original importer into the EU from a non-Member State.

4.23 Under Section 2(3) of the CPA, suppliers are also potentially liable, but only if they fail within a reasonable time to identify a person set out at Section 2(2).

4.24 For an individual claim, there could be more than one producer, because a product is defined at Section 1(2) as including 'a product which is comprised in another product, whether by virtue of being a component part or raw material or otherwise'. Thus, where the defect is in a component part of the product which is supplied to the final producer, both the manufacturer of the component part and the manufacturer of the final product will be potentially liable.

What are the statutory defences to the CPA 1987?

4.25 The six statutory defences to claims brought under the CPA 1987 are found at Section 4(1):

(a) that the defect is attributable to compliance with any requirement imposed by or under any enactment or with any EU obligation; or
(b) that the person proceeded against did not at any time supply the product to another; or
(c) that the following conditions are satisfied, that is to say—
   (i) that the only supply of the product to another by the person proceeded against was otherwise than in the course of a business of that person's; and
   (ii) that section 2(2) above[34] does not apply to that person or applies to him by virtue only of things done otherwise than with a view to profit; or
(d) that the defect did not exist in the product at the relevant time; or
(e) that the state of scientific and technical knowledge at the relevant time was not such that a producer of products of the same description as the product in question might be expected to have discovered the defect if it had existed in his products while they were under his control; or
(e) that the defect—

33 See s 1(2). Producers can also be '(b) in the case of a substance which has not been manufactured but has been won or abstracted, the person who won or abstracted it; (c) in the case of a product which has not been manufactured, won or abstracted but essential characteristics of which are attributable to an industrial or other process having been carried out (for example, in relation to agricultural produce), the person who carried out that process'.

34 I.e. that liability applies to: '(a) the producer of the product; (b) any person who, by putting his name on the product or using a trade mark or other distinguishing mark in relation to the product, has held himself out to be the producer of the product; (c) any person who has imported the product into a member State from a place outside the member States in order, in the course of any business of his, to supply it to another.'

(i) constituted a defect in a product ('the subsequent product') in which the product in question had been comprised; and
(ii) was wholly attributable to the design of the subsequent product or to compliance by the producer of the product in question with instructions given by the producer of the subsequent product.

4.26 The burden is on the defendant to establish a defence, on the balance of probabilities.

4.27 The defence at Section 4(1)(e) is known as the 'development risks defence'. Its ambit has been the subject of extensive discussion, notably in *A v NBA*.[35] In that case it was established that to invoke the defence successfully, the defect must have been not discoverable in light of the scientific and technical knowledge available to *anyone* at the time – not just the knowledge available to the defendant.[36] The defence is highly relevant to the rapidly developing field of autonomous vehicles. For example, in 2015 Chrysler announced a recall for 1.4 million vehicles after a pair of hackers demonstrated to reporters that they could remotely hijack a Jeep's digital systems over the internet, taking over dashboard functions, steering, transmission and brakes. Had such a hack been carried out maliciously and given rise to a collision, a manufacturer would need to try to show in its defence that it would not have been possible to envisage and counter the nature of the hacking at the time. For this reason, manufacturers would be well advised to keep detailed records of their state of knowledge during the development process.

4.28 As well as the 'development risks defence', there is also the related concept of the 'state of the art defence'. The latter is not listed as one of the six statutory defences at Section 4(1), but instead arises from the definition of defect itself at Section 3, namely the provision that 'nothing in this section shall require a defect to be inferred from the fact alone that the safety of a product which is supplied after that time is greater than the safety of the product in question'. This provides a certain degree of protection to older products where the next generation is safer. The 'development risks defence' seeks to protect defendants from liability for risks which could not have been foreseen at the time of supply, whereas the 'state of the art defence' ensures there is no liability simply because standards have improved since the product was first supplied.

35 *A v NBA* (n 18).

36 See also *European Commission v United Kingdom* [1997] All ER (EC) 481, (C-300/95), in which the CJEU noted that if there is one isolated opinion at the relevant time to the effect that the product is defective, the producer cannot rely on the development risks defence. The state of scientific knowledge must be identified by the most advanced level of research, not the majority of learned opinion. However, the accessibility of the scientific and technical knowledge can also be taken into account. The CJEU drew a distinction between a study of a US university published in an English-language international journal and similar research carried out by an academic in Manchuria published in a local scientific journal in Chinese. However, Burton J in *A v NBA* (n 18) noted that the Manchuria example may not always work: for instance, where the product concerned was one for which Manchuria was renowned, then research in that country might be highly relevant. Burton J preferred to use the example of an unpublished document or unpublished research not available to the general public.

Contributory negligence

4.29 The defence of contributory negligence is available under the CPA 1987. However, in the UK contributory negligence cannot be 100 per cent – see *Pitts v Hunt*.[37] This means that it cannot be used to disallow the liability completely, only as a means of reducing the liability. As to apportioning damages under contributory negligence, the Law Reform (Contributory Negligence) Act 1945 provides that the damages 'shall be reduced to such extent as the court thinks just and equitable having regard to the claimant's share in the responsibility for the damage'.[38] In practice in a defective products context, the courts will often be generous to claimants, to reflect the general policy decision to bring in 'strict liability' under the CPA 1987.

4.30 Where an automated feature fails on a vehicle and this leads to a collision, the manufacturer may seek to argue contributory negligence on the basis that the driver should have resumed control of the vehicle within a reasonable amount of time and averted the collision. However, such an argument is likely to be met by reference to the various studies which have shown that it takes the average human driver several seconds to take back control of a vehicle which has been proceeding in automated mode.[39] These considerations are likely to be highly fact-sensitive.

Limitation periods for CPA 1987 claims

4.31 The CPA 1987 provides for a ten-year 'long stop' provision, which means that a claim can only be made in the first ten years from the date of supply of the product. Unusually in the context of limitation of actions, this 'long stop' does not simply impose a procedural bar to an action to which the section applies, but extinguishes the right of action altogether. This limits the utility of the CPA 1987 in the context of vehicles which may be used for much longer than ten years. However, it does mean that generally – at least for CPA 1987 purposes – there is no need for a developer to keep records longer than ten years.

4.32 Subject to this 'long stop', property damage claims must be brought within three years from the date on which the cause of action accrued or the date of knowledge of the claimant or (if earlier) of any person in whom the cause of action was previously vested.[40] The CPA 1987 provides at Section 5(5):

> In determining…when any such loss or damage [to property] occurred, the loss or damage shall be regarded as having occurred at the earliest time at which a person with an interest in the property had knowledge of the material facts about the loss or damage.

37 [1990] 3 All ER 344.
38 Section 1(1).
39 Naughton (n 4); Eriksson and Stanton (n 4).
40 Limitation Act 1980, s 11A(4).

4.33 Similarly, personal injury claims must be brought within three years of the date on which the cause of action accrued, or (if later) the date of the knowledge of the injured person.[41] The court also has discretion to allow an action to proceed if it would be equitable to do so, even if the three-year period has passed.[42] If the injured person dies before the expiration of the limitation period, the cause of action survives for the benefit of the victim's estate. A claim can then be brought within three years of either the date of death or the date of the personal representative's knowledge.[43] Again, this is subject to the ten-year 'long stop'.

4.34 If the product causes death, dependants may be able to bring a claim under the Fatal Accidents Act 1976. If the deceased's claim was not already time-barred as at the date of his death, then a claim by a dependant can be brought within three years of whichever is the later of (i) the date of death and (ii) the date of knowledge of the person for whose benefit the action is brought.[44] Again, this is subject to the ten-year 'long stop'.

4.35 Some general provisions from the Limitation Act 1980 are also relevant to the CPA 1987, although none of them overrule the ten-year 'long stop' period. Notably, where a claimant is under a disability, an additional limitation period will start to run when that person ceases to be under a disability (or dies).[45] Similarly, there are provisions to extend the limitation period for fraud, deliberate concealment or mistake.[46]

Contractual liability

4.36 Usually the term 'product liability' is used specifically to refer to civil liability under the CPA 1987. However, claims arising from defective products may be brought for breach of contract or negligence. Claims may also be brought for misrepresentation, either at common law or under the Misrepresentation Act 1967.[47] A full discussion of these causes of action is beyond the scope of this book, but a short summary of some key points is provided.

4.37 Importantly, contractual claims may be affected by the provisions of the Sale of Goods Act 1979, the Supply of Goods and Services Act 1982 and the Consumer Rights Act 2015. The 1979 and 1982 Acts apply to all contracts entered into prior to 1 October 2015 (whether in a business or consumer context); the Consumer Rights Act 2015 includes similar provisions for consumer contracts entered into from 1 October 2015. Each of these acts creates an

---

41 Limitation Act 1980, s 11A(4).

42 Limitation Act 1980, s 33.

43 Limitation Act 1980, s 11A(5).

44 Limitation Act 1980, s 12(2).

45 Limitation Act 1980, s 28. 'Disability' has a technical meaning here, being either a claimant who is an infant or who lacks capacity within the meaning of the Mental Capacity Act 2005 to conduct legal proceedings (Limitation Act 1980, s 38(2)).

46 Limitation Act 1980, s 32.

47 Section 2(6) of the CPA 1987 provides that it shall operate 'without prejudice to any liability arising otherwise than by virtue of this Part'.

implied term that goods sold 'in the course of a business' are of 'satisfactory quality'.[48] Satisfactory quality is defined as 'the standard that a reasonable person would regard as satisfactory', taking into account any description of the goods, the cost/consideration provided and 'all other relevant circumstances'. The 1979 and 2015 Acts include a specific list of aspects to be considered in assessing satisfactory quality, including 'fitness for all the purposes for which goods of the kind in question are commonly supplied', 'appearance and finish', 'freedom from minor defects', 'safety' and 'durability'.

4.38 Liability in contract is generally strict, once breach is established – in other words, there is no need to prove an element of wrongdoing or negligence. Moreover, contractual claims can be made for pure economic losses. However, contractual claims are limited in that claims may generally only be brought where there is a direct contractual relationship between the parties – hence a pedestrian knocked down by an autonomous vehicle would not have a contractual cause of action.

4.39 The limitation period in respect of contract is generally six years from the date of breach. There are limited exceptions to this for deliberate concealment, personal injury cases and claims by persons under a disability. As contractual and negligence claims are not subject to the ten-year 'long stop' that applies to claims under the CPA 1987, in certain cases it may be that a claim under the CPA 1987 is no longer available but a contractual or negligence claim remains viable.

Negligence

4.40 Unlike contract, product liability in tort can extend beyond the contractual relationship to third parties who suffer loss. In a negligence claim, the claimant has to establish that the producer owed a duty to take reasonable care to avoid property damage or personal injury as a result of the defective product. What amounts to 'reasonable care' will be highly fact-dependant, but the courts will bear in mind that 'a car is potentially a dangerous weapon'.[49] The claimant must also prove that the breach of the duty of care caused the claimant damage.

4.41 Part of the duty of care will involve the duty to warn of non-obvious risks associated with their products. However, there is no duty to warn users of dangers which are obvious or common knowledge.[50]

4.42 There must be personal injury or damage to property other than the product supplied in order to bring a claim in negligence – there can be no claim for pure economic loss. Only foreseeable losses will be recoverable. If a consumer misuses the product in a way which could not have been foreseen by the producer, there will no liability in respect of such damage.

4.43 One issue in relation to negligence and artificial intelligence concerns the extent to which behaviour attributable to machine learning is foreseeable.

48 Sale of Goods Act 1979 s 14, Supply of Goods and Services Act 1982 s 9, Consumer Rights Act 2015 s 9 (and see also s 34 for an equivalent provision in relation to 'digital content').

49 *Lunt v Khelifa* [2002] EWCA Civ 801, [20] *per* Latham LJ.

50 See the discussion of the duty to warn in the context of the CPA, at paragraph 4.17 above.

As was stated by Thomas Burri in his paper 'Machine Learning and the Law: Five Theses':

> The behaviour and actions of machine learning systems are not fully foreseeable in all situations, even when the algorithm directing the learning is known. A machine learning system's behaviour is based on the patterns and correlations it discovers in datasets. These patterns and correlations by nature are not known in advance, else no learning would be required.[51]

This is unlikely to present a substantial obstacle to recovery of damages in a negligence action arising out of a road traffic accident involving an autonomous vehicle, since it is not necessary to show that the defendant should have foreseen precisely what happened; it is enough if the injury is of a type that could have been foreseen even if it came about in an unexpected way. However, this point raises potentially interesting questions about the nature of reasonable care and skill in a context whereby the rationale of a vehicle's behaviour may not be fully understood even by those manufacturing it. As Matthew Lavy argues in his article 'Reasonable Skill and Care in the Age of Machine Learning: Some Preliminary Thoughts':

> The focus shifts from actually producing artefacts to designing and implementing quality control processes; exercising reasonable skill and care involves ensuring that the level of scrutiny of which the outputs of machine learning algorithms are subjected is commensurate with the risks involved in the exercise and the ramifications of failure.[52]

Given that the risks involved in putting vehicles on public roads are very substantial, the level of scrutiny which the courts will expect of the machine learning outputs will likely be equally substantial. However, in a specifically autonomous vehicle context, in most cases the type of damage – injury to other road users, pedestrians and property – will likely be sufficiently foreseeable to give rise for liability for that damage, even if the precise mechanism is not.

4.44 The limitation period in respect of negligence is generally six years from when the damage is first sustained. There is a special time limit of three years from the date of knowledge for claims in tort where facts relevant to the cause of action are not known at the date of accrual of the cause of action;[53] this is subject to an overriding time limit of 15 years.[54] In the case of fraud, the period of limitation does not begin to run at all until the claimant has or could have discovered the fraud with reasonable diligence.[55] There is a shorter time limit of three years for claims involving personal injuries. As for contract, it is perfectly possible that a valid negligence claim may subsist even after a claim under the CPA 1987 has become time-barred by the ten-year 'long stop'.

51 www.mlandthelaw.org/papers/burri.pdf, accessed 27 August 2018.
52 *Computers and Law Magazine*, August/September 2017.
53 Limitation Act 1980, s 14A.
54 Limitation Act 1980, s 14B.
55 Limitation Act 1980, s 32.

CHAPTER 5

Cyber security and data protection

Matthew Channon

Introduction

5.1 Cyber security and data protection are undoubtedly a significant challenge for both connected vehicles[1] and autonomous vehicles. Notoriously, in 2015 a pair of security researchers found a way to gain remote access to a Jeep Cherokee and take control of the engine, brakes and entertainment system.[2] This prompted the recall of 1.4 million vehicles.[3] Moreover, concerns surround the potential for 'ransomware' attacks along the lines of the 'WannaCry' virus which paralysed the NHS in May 2017. Equally, the possibility for terrorist incidents is obvious. At a more mundane level, 'smart' cars are capable of gathering a great deal of sensitive data – for example, about how often users go to the gym or where they worship – and it is important that this is safeguarded.

5.2 Although to date no physical injury or damage has been caused by hacking of autonomous vehicles, the potential stakes are high.[4] Furthermore, the interconnected nature of autonomous vehicles provides a potential risk in terms of the hacking of more than one vehicle at once.[5] Importantly, although commercial autonomous vehicles are some way off, connected vehicles are already routinely in production today, with a predicted 150–200 million connected vehicles on the road by 2020.[6]

1 In terms of the relationship between the terms 'connected' and 'autonomous' vehicles, the Society of Motor Manufacturers and Traders noted, 'Vehicles with some levels of automation do not necessarily need to be connected, and vice versa, although the two technologies can be complementary. Technology convergence, however, will result in intelligent vehicles that are both connected and autonomous, hence connected and autonomous vehicles (CAVs)'. See Society of Motor Manufacturers and Traders, 'Connected and Autonomous Vehicles: Position Paper' (February 2017), 5, www.smmt.co.uk/wp-content/uploads/sites/2/SMMT-CAV-position paper final.pdf, accessed 31 August 2018.

2 Andy Greenberg, 'Hackers remotely kill a Jeep on the highway – with me in it', www.wired.com/2015/07/hackers-remotely-kill-jeep-highway, accessed 28 August 2018.

3 'Fiat Chrysler recalls 1.4 million cars after Jeep hack', www.bbc.co.uk/news/technology-3365049, accessed 28 August 2018.

4 Daniel J. Fagnant and Kara Kockleman, 'Preparing a nation for autonomous vehicles: opportunities, barriers and policy recommendations' (2015) *Transportation Research Part A: Policy and Practice*, 178.

5 Tim Ring, 'Connected cars – the next target for hackers' (2015) *Network Security*, No. 11, November 2015, 11–16, 12.

6 Ibid.

5.3 Moreover, the amount of highly sensitive personal data within these vehicles, through audio/visual recordings, telematics data, and personal information,[7] is highly attractive to external stakeholders who want to use this personal data in a variety of ways such as through the pricing of premiums[8] or through the assessment of legal liability for collisions.[9] Data is also a significant attraction for cyber hackers.

5.4 The potential for cyber security breaches has a significant impact on public perception. A survey conducted internationally by Kyriakidis et al. of 5,000 individuals found the most apprehension surrounded the potential for software hacking and misuse.[10] Moreover, businesses and manufacturers also have the potential for significant economic loss through loss of productivity due to autonomous vehicle hacks[11] as well as the potential for significant liability claims due to injury or damage caused by hacked vehicles.

5.5 It is clear that there is a lot at stake in ensuring that autonomous vehicles are secure against the risk of cyber security attacks, and the question arises as to how the law is currently reacting to these challenges. Moreover, autonomous vehicles raise considerable privacy concerns surrounding data and data ownership. This chapter will first examine the UK, EU and US regulation of cyber security as well as liability resulting from cyber attacks, before going on to consider matters relating to the hacking of data, data protection and data access.

Regulation of cyber security (physical)

5.6 The legal response to the cyber security challenges of autonomous vehicles has been substantial. Attempts have been made at international level to ensure that cyber security rules do not conflict, and that there is an overall global standard for cyber security. As noted by the House of Lords Science and Technology Committee: 'An international effort is necessary to tackle the risks associated with cybersecurity, which are likely to rise – especially on a global scale.'[12] At an EU level, the Directive on the Security of Network

---

7 Hazel Si Min Lim and Araz Taeihagh, 'Autonomous Vehicles for Smart ad Sustainable Cities: An In-Depth Exploration of Privacy and Cybersecurity Implications' (2018) *Energies*, Vol. 11, No. 5, 1062, https://arxiv.org/abs/1804.10367, accessed 30 August 2018.

8 Lloyds of London, 'Autonomous vehicles: Handing Over Control: Opportunities and Risks for Insurance' (2014), 21, www.lloyds.com/news-and-risk-insight/risk-reports/library/technology/autonomous-vehicles, accessed 29 August 2018.

9 The insurance industry would like access of autonomous vehicle data to determine whether the vehicle was 'driving itself' for the purposes of the Automated and Electric Vehicles Act. See paragraph 3.31.

10 M. Kyriakidis, R. Happee and J.C.F.de Winter, 'Public opinion on automated driving: Results of an international questionnaire among 5000 respondents' (2015) *Transportation Research Part F: Traffic Psychology and Behaviour*, Vol. 32, 127, 133.

11 Estimated $3 trillion in lost productivity due to cyber security breaches in all areas of cyber space by 2020. Si Min Lim (n 7), 11.

12 House of Lords Science and Technology Select Committee, *Connected and Autonomous Vehicles: The future?* (HL 2016-16, HL 115), 8.

and Information Systems (NIS Directive)[13] was introduced 'to achieve a high common level of security of network and information systems within the Union'.[14] Article 7(1) of the Directive states:

> Each Member State shall adopt a national strategy on the security of network and information systems defining the strategic objectives and appropriate policy and regulatory measures with a view to achieving and maintaining a high level of security of network and information systems.

The Directive further requires Member States to 'designate one or more national competent authorities on the security of network and information systems'.[15]

5.7 Further efforts have been made at to introduce guidelines and resources to ensure that there is a global standard for cyber security. As will be noted later in this chapter, the Society of Automotive Engineers (SAE) has developed a guidebook (J3061) on Cyber-Physical Vehicle Systems,[16] and the Society of Global Automakers has further developed guidelines.[17] The United Nations Economic Commission for Europe (UNECE) has also been prevalent in this area through the introduction of Cyber Security Guidelines in March 2017.[18]

5.8 The UK is also taking steps towards protection of cyber security. The House of Lords Science and Technology Committee noted that 'Cybersecurity should also form an integral part of the Government's review of the regulatory framework for CAV'[19] and further that the Centre for Connected and Autonomous Vehicles (CCAV) should take a coordinating role in this area.[20] At an international level, the DfT is working with the United Nations to develop international requirements[21] and furthermore through its joint chairmanship (with Japan) of a task force on cyber security.[22] This task force is due to submit recommendations to World Forum for the Harmonisation of Vehicle Standards in 2018.[23]

5.9 At national level, the UK has introduced two pieces of regulation aimed at manufacturers and testers of autonomous vehicles: first, through

---

13 Directive (EU) 2016/1148 of the European Parliament and of the Council of 6 July 2016 concerning measures for a high common level of security of network and information systems across the Union (2016) OJ L 194.

14 Ibid., Article 1(1).

15 Ibid., Article 8(1).

16 Association of Automotive Engineers, 'Cybersecurity Guidebook for Cyber-Physical Vehicle Systems' (2012), www.sae.org/standards/content/j3061, accessed 30 August 2018.

17 Society of Global Automakers, 'Framework for Automotive Cyber Security Best Practices' (January 2016), www.globalautomakers.org/OldSiteContentAssets/press-release/Automakers-Develop-Framework-for-Automotive-Cybersecurity-Best-Practices-assets/framework-autocyberbestpractices-14jan20161 pdf, accessed 28 August 2018.

18 UNECE, 'Proposal for draft guidelines on cyber security and data protection Submitted by the Informal Working Group on Intelligent Transport Systems/Automated Driving' (March 2017).

19 House of Lords Science and Technology Select Committee (n 12), 8.

20 Ibid.

21 See Letter from the Minister of State the Rt Hon. John Hayes CBE MP to the Automated and Electric Vehicle Bill Committee (16 November 2017), http://data.parliament.uk/DepositedPapers/Files/DEP2017-0702/Letter_to_Committee_-_Adding_word_securely_to_Clause_1.pdf> accessed 28 August 2018.

22 Ibid.

23 Ibid.

the introduction of 'The Pathway to Driverless Cars: A Code of Practice for testing' (the Code of Practice)[24] in July 2015, containing key vehicular requirements on cyber security where an autonomous vehicle is being tested; and, second, through the introduction of more detailed 'key principles of vehicle cyber security for connected and automated vehicles' (the Key Principles)[25] in August 2017. Both the Code of Practice and the Key Principles are flexible non-statutory instruments, and there are no requirements, per se, for manufacturer or vehicle tester to follow them.[26] However, as noted in the Code of Practice, a failure to follow the Code may be relevant to liability in legal proceedings.[27] Both the Code of Practice and Key Principles are not fixed and will likely be adapted over time depending on the development of cyber security threats as well as the development of the technology.

UK

Testing

5.10 The Code of Practice provides only limited guidance in relation to cyber security. Paragraph 5.14 notes that manufacturers and suppliers of parts for test vehicles will need to ensure that vehicles have appropriate levels of security built in them. Moreover, vehicles that are being tested must have a test driver or operator overseeing the movements of the vehicle who is capable of manually overriding at any time (para 5.13). Rather than providing detail, para 5.15 of the Code of Practice refers to the security principles contained within the BSI PAS754 Software Trustworthiness – Governance and management – Specification. PAS754 was launched by the Government to help manufacturers avoid software failures and is seen as the UK's 'first successful attempt at codifying what constitutes good software engineering'.[28] It is not aimed specifically at autonomous vehicle technology but at software generally, as part of the UK's Cyber Security Strategy.[29] Interestingly, the Code does not provide guidance into data hacking, although it does contain a section on data protection, emphasising the need to comply with the Data Protection Act 1998.[30]

24 'The Pathway to Driverless Cars: A Code of Practice for testing' (Department for Transport, July 2015), www.gov.uk/government/publications/automated-vehicle-technologies-testing-code-of-practice, accessed 27 August 2018.

25 'The key principles of vehicle cyber security for connected and automated vehicles' (Department for Transport, August 2017), www.gov.uk/government/publications/principles-of-cyber-security-for-connected-and-automated-vehicles/the-key-principles-of-vehicle-cyber-security-for-connected-and-automated-vehicles, accessed 27 August 2018.

26 As to the relevance of the Code of Practice to legal liability, see paragraph 2.14.

27 Code of Practice for Testing (n 24), [1.5].

28 'The UK Cyber Security Strategy Report on Progress and Forward Plans' (Cabinet Office, December 2014), 5.

29 For more detail on the UK Cyber Security Strategy, see ibid. and 'The UK Cyber Security Strategy: Protecting and promoting the UK in a digital world' (Cabinet Office, November 2011), https://assets.publishing.service.gov.uk/government/uploads/system/uploads/attachment_data/file/60961/uk-cyber-security-strategy-final.pdf, accessed 29 August 2018.

30 Succeeded by the Data Protection Act 2018 as will be discussed later.

5.11 The Key Principles offer much greater detail in the protection of cyber security. The rationale for the introduction of these principles is to provide all parties involved in the manufacturing of autonomous vehicles with a 'consistent set of guidelines'.[31]

Personal accountability

5.12 One of the core themes within the Key Principles concerns engagement and collective responsibility throughout the manufacturing supply chain and at all company levels. For example, as noted in Principle 1.2,[32] 'personal accountability is held at board level for product and system security'. Personal accountability is clearly not just in relation to autonomous vehicles but in all areas of cyber security. As noted by James, 'No longer can security be viewed as a prohibited silo residing outside of key boardroom discussions, adhering to a self-generated checklist of things that must be implemented'.[33] Furthermore, another significant requirement is for both awareness and training to ensure that there is a 'culture of security to ensure that individuals know their role and responsibilities' (Principle 1.3).[34] Again however, little detail is provided as to who in the organisation requires training and the specific training that is required. Further, organisations must engage with appropriate third parties, and within themselves to ensure that they are aware of cyber threats and have appropriate responses.[35]

Lifetime maintenance

5.13 Significant attention is further given to ensuring that products are secure throughout their lifetime (see Principle 3). James notes that, 'Ultimately, it's important to understand that the exponential growth of technology has meant the foundations of security practices are evolving at a rapid pace'.[36] Principle 3.1 of the Key Principles provides that, 'Organisations plan for how to maintain security over the lifetime of their systems'. Manufacturers must also 'safely and securely'[37] update software if it becomes corrupt.

5.14 Of course, as noted in the chapter about insurance (paras 3.34–3.39), the Automated and Electric Vehicles Act (AEVA 2018) aids manufacturers' software updates, by allowing the vehicle's insurer to refuse compensation or recover compensation from the insured if 'safety-critical software' is not updated.[38]

31 Key Principles (n 25), introduction.
32 Key Principles (n 25).
33 Lee James, 'Making cyber-security a strategic business priority' (2018) *Network Security*, No. 5, 6–9, 6.
34 Key Principles (n 25).
35 Ibid., Principle 2.2.
36 Lee James (n 33), 8.
37 Key Principles (n 25), Principle 6.3.
38 Section 4(1) (exclude) and Section 4(4) (recover) of the Automated and Electric Vehicles Act.

International guidelines

5.15 A number of organisations and bodies internationally have focussed on providing manufacturers with the necessary guidelines for best practice, and design principles. For example, the Global Automakers framework[39] for cyber security best practices, providing flexibility to manufacturers 'to permit implementation in a manner consistent with the unique needs and circumstances of individual companies'.[40] The framework is comprised of practices such as 'vehicle security by design'[41] (the need to ensure that cyber security is considered throughout the design of the vehicle) and 'incident response and recovery' (an incident response plan to document process in responding to cyber security incidents).[42] The SAE, on the other hand, published the SAE J3061 'Recommended Best Practice, Cybersecurity Guidebook for Cyber-Physical Vehicle Systems'[43] in January 2016, which provides standards on automotive cyber security. The Guidebook sets out the ways to implement a cyber security process framework for security critical information systems.[44]

5.16 The UNECE is also prevalent in this area and has adopted – as part of the *Consolidated Resolution on the Construction of Vehicles*[45] – guidelines on cyber security and data protection.[46] The guidelines are again very broad, allowing flexibility as to how they are to be achieved. For example: 'Automotive manufacturers, component/system suppliers and service providers must ensure that there is adequate protection against manipulation and misuse both of the technical structure and of the data and processes.'[47] The means by which this protection is achieved is not specified.[48] As noted by the UNECE, the guidelines produced and inserted in the Resolution are only interim until the development of more globally harmonised requirements.[49] It is evident that the number of different guidelines available from a number of organisations

39 Association of Global Automakers, 'Framework for Automotive Cyber Security Best Practices' (n 16), 2.

40 Ibid.

41 Ibid., 4.

42 Ibid., 5.

43 Society of Automotive Engineers, 'Recommended Best Practice, Cybersecurity Guidebook for Cyber-Physical Vehicle Systems (J3061)' (n 16).

44 www.sae.org/news/2017/03/sae-j3061-guidebook-helping-to-frame-cybersecurity-policy, accessed 30 August 2018.

45 Economic Commission for Europe (UNECE), Inland Transport Committee World Forum for Harmonization of Vehicle Regulations, Consolidated Resolution on the Construction of Vehicles (July 2017) (UNECE Resolution).

46 Ibid., Annexe 6.

47 Ibid., 114.

48 For example, through the International Organisation for Standardization (ISO)/International Electrotechnical Commission (IEC) 15408-1:2009, which 'establishes the general concepts and principles of IT security evaluation and specifies the general model of evaluation given by various parts of ISO/IEC 15408 which in its entirety is meant to be used as the basis for evaluation of security properties of IT products': see ISO/IEC 15408-1:2009 'Information technology – Security techniques – Evaluation criteria for IT security – Part 1: Introduction and general model', www.iso.org/standard/50341.html, accessed 29 August 2018.

49 UNECE Resolution (n 45), 114.

is likely to cause confusion, and therefore, at least prior to the introduction of more advanced autonomous vehicles, global requirements are necessary.

US NHTSA guidance

5.17 The US regime for cyber security of autonomous vehicles is very much based on guidance compared to legislation.[50] This has been a collaborative effort, with both law makers and vehicle manufacturers involved. In particular, the National Highway Traffic Safety Administration (NHTSA) has been proactive in its attempts to collaborate with manufacturers. For example, 'Proactive Safety Principles' were introduced jointly by manufacturers and the NHTSA, with one of the objectives being to 'explore and employ ways to work collaboratively in order to mitigate those cyber threats that could present unreasonable safety risks'.[51] One of the ways to do this was to 'develop appropriate means for engaging with cybersecurity researchers as an additional tool for cyber threat identification and remedy'.[52] The NHTSA has further encouraged motor vehicle manufacturers to form an ISAC (Information Sharing and Analysis Centre) allowing manufacturers to 'proactively and uniformly address cyber security weaknesses';[53] this was eventually formed in 2015.[54]

5.18 In its 'Federal Automated Vehicles Policy',[55] the NHTSA iterated the importance of cyber secure vehicles, and stated that manufacturers should 'follow a robust product development process based on a systems-engineering approach to minimise risks to safety…including cyber security'.[56] Much of this was based on ensuring that manufacturers and suppliers follow and incorporate guidance from a number of organisations and administrations, both national and international, including the NHTSA, the Society of Automotive Engineers (SAE International) and the Association of Global Automakers.[57]

5.19 Within the US, the National Institute of Standards and Technology has further released its own Framework for Improving Critical Infrastructure Cyber Security, recently updated in April 2018.[58] As the title suggests, this addresses

50 Although note that there have been two attempts in the US to introduce legislation in relation to cyber security and privacy. The Security and Privacy in Your Car Act (Spy Car Act 2015) (S.1806 – 114th Congress (2015–2016)) and the Security and Privacy in Your Car Act 2017 (Spy Car Act 2017) (S.680 –115th Congress (2017–2018)). The Spy Car Act 2015 was sent to the Committee on Commerce, Science, and Transportation but was not passed. The Spy Car Act of 2017 was then introduced with focus on both cyber security (Section 2) and privacy (Section 4); it was referred to the Committee on Commerce, Science, and Transportation and is yet to be passed.

51 NHTSA et al., 'Proactive Safety Principles 2016', 3, www.transportation.gov/briefing-room/proactive-safety-principles-2016, accessed 28 August 2018.

52 Ibid.

53 NHTSA, 'NHTSA and Vehicle Cyber Security' (2016), 5, www.nhtsa.gov/sites/nhtsa.dot.gov/files/documents/nhtsavehiclecybersecurity2016.pdf, accessed 28 August 2018.

54 See www.automotiveisac.com, accessed 31 August 2018.

55 NHTSA, 'Federal Automated Vehicles Policy' (2016), www.nhtsa.gov/sites/nhtsa.dot.gov/files/federal_automated_vehicles_policy.pdf, accessed 28 August 2018.

56 Ibid., 20.

57 Ibid., 21.

58 National Institute of Standards and Technology, 'Framework for Improving Critical Infrastructure Cybersecurity' (Version 1.1, 2018).

critical infrastructure, rather than specifically autonomous vehicles. It is used to 'help identify and prioritize actions for reducing cybersecurity risk, and… aligning policy, business, and technological approaches to managing that risk'.[59] The approach is structured around five functions – 'Identify, Protect, Detect, Respond, and Recover'[60] – of a successful cyber security programme and provides greater detail as to how to undertake these. For example, in 'protect', the organisation's personnel and partners are provided with cyber security awareness education and are trained to perform duties related to cyber security.[61]

NHTSA Best Practice vs the UK Key Principles

5.20 Finally, the NHTSA released the 'Cyber Security Best Practice for Modern Vehicles' (CSBP)[62] in October 2016, a voluntary set of best practice guidelines to provide 'a solid foundation for developing a risk-based approach and important processes that can be maintained, refreshed and updated effectively over time to serve the needs of the automotive industry'.[63] The CSBP is comparable to the UK Key Principles,[64] as discussed earlier in this chapter. One of the key provisions within the CSBP is around the need to follow a 'robust product development process based on a systems engineering process',[65] with the goal of 'designing systems free of unreasonable safety risks'.[66] This is undoubtedly similar to the provision in the UK Key Principles which focus on 'security by design' (Principle 1.4), with security integrated within the product development process. Where a cyber attack is detected, mitigation is required in relation to the safety risk to vehicle occupants and pedestrians with the vehicle transitioned to a 'reasonable risk state'[67] with information collected by the automotive industry and shared through an Auto ISAC.[68] This again is similar to the UK Key Principles which require 'incident response plans in place' (Principle 3.2). At the opposite end of the spectrum and similar to Principle 6 of the Key Principles, the CSBP provides that 'this process (to evaluate risks) should give explicit considerations to privacy and cybersecurity risks through the entire life-cycle of the vehicle'.[69]

5.21 Further, the CSBP centres on the need for a 'culture' that is prepared to 'handle increasing cybersecurity challenges'.[70] This could be through 'developing or integrating safety-critical vehicle systems [that] prioritize vehicle

59 Ibid., 6.
60 Ibid.
61 Ibid., 31.
62 NHTSA, 'Cybersecurity Best Practices for Modern Vehicle, (2016), www.nhtsa.gov/sites/nhtsa.dot.gov/files/documents/812333_cybersecurityformodernvehicles.pdf, accessed 29 August 2018.
63 Ibid., 5.
64 Key Principles (n 25).
65 NHTSA (n 62), 12.
66 Ibid.
67 Ibid.
68 Ibid.
69 Ibid.
70 Ibid.

cybersecurity'.[71] Falling short on the UK Key Principles, which provide the need for 'personal accountability', the CSBP encourages a 'top-down emphasis',[72] which the NHTSA argues 'demonstrates the seriousness of the organization in managing cyber security risks.'[73]

Compensatory regime for cyber security breaches

5.22 The mode of compensation of damage victims where a cyber security breach occurs is unclear. The coverage of cyber attacks within the Automated and Electric Vehicles Act 2018 (AEVA 2018) will depend on the Act's interpretation of the term 'driving itself', a requisite of Section 2(1). As noted by Section 8(1)(a) AEVA 2018, 'a vehicle is "driving itself" if it is operating in a mode in which it is not being controlled, and does not need to be monitored, by an individual'. It is questionable whether such a term would encompass hacking scenarios as there is no clarification of who an 'individual' is. Consequently, the vehicle could be being 'controlled' or 'monitored' by an individual, albeit the vehicle hacker. This would be something likely left to the courts to decide or through the provision of later clarity. Importantly, Section 2(6) of the Act prevents restrictions or limitations within the policy, meaning that an insurer cannot contractually exclude compensation for cyber attacks.

5.23 Of course, under Section 4(1) of the AEVA 2018, the insurer is able to limit or exclude liability under their policy against the insured for failure to update 'safety-critical software' or for prohibited software alterations. Moreover, the insurer is able to recover damages paid from the insured for the same (Section 4(4) AEVA 2018). Insurers are able to recover damages from the manufacturer or any other liable person for damage caused as a result of the vehicle driving itself (Section 5(1) AEVA 2018). If, for example, manufacturers could not have foreseen a potential loophole in their security systems when designed, then there is potential for use of the 'state of the art' defence.[74] Even without the coverage of the AEVA 2018, there is potential for manufacturers to compensate the victim under product liability, although this is complex and subject to the 'state of the art' defence (as discussed in Chapter 4).

5.24 A potential route to cyber hacking compensation could be through the extension of one of the pre-existing funds available, either Pool Reinsurance (Pool Re) or the MIB Agreements. Pool Re could already cover for certain losses as a result of terrorism.[75] In April 2018, the remit of the fund was extended to cover for

71 Ibid., 13.

72 Ibid.

73 Ibid.

74 'State of the art' defence is contained in Section 4(1)(e) Consumer Protection Act 1987.

75 This was in light of the bombing of the Baltic Exchange. Insurers were withdrawing cover for terrorist losses in the early 1990s. Terrorism is defined in Section 2(2) of the Reinsurance (Acts of Terrorism) Act 1993 as 'acts of persons acting on behalf of, or in connection with, any organisation which carries out activities directed towards the overthrowing or influencing, by force or violence, of Her Majesty's government in the United Kingdom or any other government de jure or de facto'.

cyber terrorism due to the potential 'extensive repercussions' of a cyber terrorist incident.[76] The members of Pool Re are major property insurers, who pay losses for the insured property up to a certain threshold and then claim money from Pool Re reserves thereafter. If Pool Re reserves are also exhausted, then the rest of the compensation is paid by Parliament.[77] Pool Re is limited to commercial property damage, meaning that it does not cover personal injury losses or private property.[78] Such an extension of Pool Re to cover for personal injury is not difficult to envisage; however, the combination of both commercial property damage and personal injury in the same fund, may cause a significant challenge in terms of funding. Another option could be through the Motor Insurers' Bureau (MIB) Uninsured Drivers' Agreement (UDA)[79] which could be extended to cover autonomous vehicle cyber attacks. The MIB, until recently, restricted compensation paid to victims of terrorism through its UDA;[80] the removal of this provision could therefore mean the MIB compensating in this situation and manufacturers could be required to contribute to this fund. However, unlike conventional motor insurance where the insurer is able to contractually restrict compensation claims due to terrorism (it is not a prohibited clause in Section 148 (2) RTA 1988), which would mean the claim falling to the MIB, the AEVA 2018 currently restricts exclusion clauses from being used by the insurer (Section 2(6) AEVA 2018). An alteration would therefore be required to the AEVA 2018 for the MIB to step in. Further, the MIB, under Article 75 of its Articles of Association, could require the insurer to compensate anyway as its agent.[81]

5.25 The mode of compensation in relation to cyber breaches 'across an entire vehicle fleet'[82] is unclear. The potential for a 'chilling effect' on innovation, if such compensation was left to manufacturers,[83] is worthy of future study.

76 Pool Re, 'Pool Re to extend cover to include physical damage from cyber terrorism from April 2018', www.poolre.co.uk/pool-re-extend-cover-include-physical-damage-cyber-terrorism-april-2018, accessed 29 August 2018.

77 Under Section 1(1) Reinsurance (Acts of Terrorism) Act 1993.

78 Pool Re: Terrorism: Written question – 108926 (October 2017).

79 Motor Insurers Bureau, 'Uninsured Drivers' Agreement' (2015).

80 Article 9 of the MIB Uninsured Drivers' Agreement 2015 stated that 'MIB is not liable for any claim, or any part of a claim, where the death, bodily injury or damage to property was caused by, or in the course of, an act of terrorism within the meaning of section 1 of the Terrorism Act 2000'; this was removed by the MIB Uninsured Drivers' Supplementary Agreement in 2017, Article 3.

81 See Motor Insurers' Bureau, 'Articles of Association of Motor Insurers' Bureau' (2018), www.mib.org.uk/media/423529/mib-articles-of-association-19-july-2018.pdf, accessed 28 August 2018.

82 The 'an entire vehicle fleet' is a term which was used by the ABI and Thatcham Research, who stated that 'a crucial distinction will be between potential cyber breaches affecting individual vehicles and "systemic" attacks across an entire vehicle fleet'. Association of British Insurers and Thatcham Research, 'Lords Science and Technology Select Committee inquiry on Autonomous Vehicles ABI and Thatcham Research Joint Response' (October 2016), 9.

83 The 'chilling effect' was discussed in paragraph 3.33 of this book in relation to insurer recovery against manufacturers with reference to the Schellekens article which discusses the 'chilling' effect of liability law for autonomous vehicles. Maurice Schellekens, 'Self-driving cars and the chilling effect of liability law' (2015) *Computer Law & Security Review*, Vol. 31, No. 4, 506–517, [4.2.2].

Moreover, the ABI and Thatcham Research noted that 'if adequate alternative measures are not established, this could make providing insurance for automated vehicles unattractive or even entirely unviable'.[84] The mode of compensation here, therefore, it is submitted, should be subject to further future study.

UK and EU personal data protection and security

5.26 The amount of data which will come from an autonomous vehicle is potentially enormous. As noted by the Freedom of Information and Privacy Association, 'A major technological advancement underlying the development of Connected Cars is the phenomenon known as "Big Data".'[85] Big data is used to describe the 'collection and analysis of data on a scale or of a complexity that makes the use of such data challenging'.[86] Moreover, even much smaller datasets involving a smaller number of vehicles are very valuable not only in ensuring that vehicles function properly, but also in terms of the advertisement of services to individuals using the autonomous vehicle.[87]

5.27 Threats exist around the use or the misuse of data, whether large or small, as well as the breach of privacy of autonomous vehicle users. Significant questions also surround ownership and access to vehicle and passenger data. For example, as noted in Chapter 3,[88] the insurance industry is eager to have access to accident data to enable it to determine whether the vehicle was driving itself for the purposes of the AEVA 2018.

5.28 The protection of this data, and as far as possible the privacy of vehicle users, is a key challenge both nationally and internationally. In its May 2018 Communication, the European Commission noted: 'It is also essential to find the right balance between sharing public and private data, enabling fair and effective competition for innovative solutions, and data protection.'[89] Although the EU has not directly regulated solely for autonomous vehicles, it has been active in the area of data protection, privacy and security, both in relation to transport and more generally. For example, the E Privacy Directive[90] was introduced to harmonise the laws of Member States to 'ensure an equivalent level of protection of fundamental rights and freedoms, and in particular the right to privacy,

---

84 ABI and Thatcham (n 82), 9.

85 FIPA, 'The Connected Car: Who is in the Driver's Seat?' (2018), https://fipa.bc.ca/wordpress/wp-content/uploads/2018/01/CC_report_lite.pdf, accessed 29 August 2018. The study on page 42 discusses the connected aspects of 'autonomous cars'.

86 House of Commons Science and Technology Committee, *The big data dilemma* (HC 2015–16, HC 468), 7.

87 James M. Anderson et al., *Autonomous Vehicle Technology: A Guide for Policy Makers* (RAND Corporation 2016), 94.

88 Paragraph 3.31.

89 European Commission, 'Communication from the Commission to the European Parliament, the Council, the European Economic and Social Committee, the Committee of the Regions: On the road to automated mobility: An EU strategy for mobility of the future', Brussels, 17.5.2018 COM (2018) 283 final, 2.

90 Directive 2002/58/EC of the European Parliament and of the Council of 12 July 2002 concerning the processing of personal data and the protection of privacy in the electronic communications sector (Directive on privacy and electronic communications) (2002) OJ L 201.

with respect to the processing of personal data in the electronic communication sector'.[91] This Directive deals with issues such as the erasing or anonymisation of traffic data 'when it is no longer needed for the purpose of the transmission of a communication'.[92] Furthermore, the Directive on the Framework for Deployment of Intelligent Transport Systems (IT-S)[93] was introduced in 2010, with significant data protection and privacy provisions. In particular, the Directive noted that anonymisation should be encouraged in order to protect the privacy of individuals.[94] Further, the EU is looking to adopt a delegated regulation by the end of 2018 under the ITS Directive 'to ensure secured and trustful communications between vehicles and infrastructure, sound data protection level in compliance with the General Data Protection Regulation'.[95]

5.29 The General Data Protection Regulation (GDPR) became law in 2018 with a broad mandate in the regulation of personal data. This was later implemented by the UK through the Data Protection Act 2018 (DPA). In the UK, it is the Information Commissioner's Office (ICO) which is responsible for the promotion and enforcement of the DPA. The ICO has already undertaken discussions and initial work with manufacturers and other parties in order to understand potential data protection challenges associated with the technology, and has noted its eagerness to engage with policy makers 'to help address these challenges at an early stage in order that privacy protections are "designed in"'.[96]

Data security

5.30 The Key Principles provide detail relating to the storage and transmission of personal data. Principle 7.1[97] states that data must be 'sufficiently secure' when it is stored and transmitted, 'so that only the intended recipient or system functions are able to receive and / or access it'. Further, personally identifiable data must be managed in an appropriate way (Principle 7.2),[98] and 'users are able to delete sensitive data' (Principle 7.3).[99] These principles provide clear guidance as to the importance of ensuring that user data within the car is secure. Personal data security is a challenge facing all cars with connectivity.

---

91 Ibid., Article 1(1).

92 Ibid., Article 6(1).

93 Directive 2010/40/EU of the European Parliament and of the Council of 7 July 2010 on the framework for the deployment of Intelligent Transport Systems in the field of road transport and for interfaces with other modes of transport (2010) OJ L 207. As noted, Recital 4 of the Directive: 'ITS integrate telecommunications, electronics and information technologies with transport engineering in order to plan, design, operate, maintain and manage transport

94 Ibid., Recital 13.

95 European Commission (n 89), 10.

96 Information Commissioner's Office, 'The Information Commissioner's response to the Centre for Connected and Autonomous Vehicles consultation "Pathway to Driverless Cars"' (2016), 2, https://ico.org.uk/media/about-the-ico/consultation-responses/2016/1624999/dft-pathway-to-driverless-cars-ico-response-20160909.pdf, accessed 30 August 2018.

97 Key Principles (n 25).

98 Ibid.

99 Ibid.

The management of this data 'will be essential to the wide embrace of connected cars and the data they collect'.[100]

5.31 It is further important to note in relation to the hacking and protection of data that, under the GDPR,[101] manufacturers can be held liable, in principle, for personal data loss. Further, as noted in Article 32 of the GDPR, 'the controller and the processor (of the data) shall implement appropriate technical and organisational measures to ensure a level of security appropriate to the risk'. This should include, *inter alia*, 'the ability to ensure the ongoing confidentiality, integrity, availability and resilience of processing systems and services'.[102] Where data has been breached, the controller needs to notify both the supervisory authority[103] and the data subject of this breach.[104] Article 35(1) of the GDPR states that where new technologies are likely to 'result in a high risk to the rights and freedoms of natural persons', the data controller will undertake an impact assessment of processing operations on the protection of personal data. A data protection impact assessment (DPIA) is 'an instrument to identify and analyse risks for individuals, which exist due to the use of a certain technology or system by an organization in their various roles'.[105]

Protection of 'personal data'

5.32 The GDPR is concerned primarily with 'personal data' defined in Article 4 as:

> any information relating to an identified or identifiable natural person ('data subject'); an identifiable natural person is one who can be identified, directly or indirectly, in particular by reference to an identifier such as a name, an identification number, location data, an online identifier or to one or more factors specific to the physical, physiological, genetic, mental, economic, cultural or social identity of that natural person.

5.33 Although this definition provides some clarity, there is a fine line between personal and technical data. The Court of Justice of the European

100 The Future of Privacy Forum, 'The Connected Car and Privacy: Navigating New Data Issues' (13 November 2014), 12, https://fpf.org/wp-content/uploads/FPF_Data-Collection-and-the-Connected-Car_November2014.pdf, accessed 31 August 2018.

101 Regulation (EU) 2016/679 of the European Parliament and of the Council of 27 April 2016 on the protection of natural persons with regard to the processing of personal data and on the free movement of such data, and repealing Directive 95/46/EC (General Data Protection Regulation) (2016) OJ L 119.

102 GDPR Article 32(1)(b).

103 GDPR Article 33(1); see Article 34 for 'Rules on the Establishment of Supervisory Authorities'.

104 GDPR Article 34(1): 'When the personal data breach is likely to result in a high risk to the rights and freedoms of natural persons, the controller shall communicate the personal data breach to the data subject without undue delay.'

105 Felix Bieker et al., 'A Process for Data Protection Impact Assessment Under the European General Data Protection Regulation' (2016) in Schiffner et al., 'Privacy Technologies and Policy', 4th Annual Privacy Forum, APF 2016, Frankfurt/Main, Germany, 7–8 September 2016, Proceedings, 21.

Union seemingly extended the scope of the classification of personal data further in *Breyer v Federal Republic of Germany*[106] by stating that the term 'indirectly'[107] suggests that 'it is not necessary that information alone allows the data subject to be identified'[108] and that it is not necessary that all of the information of the data subject is held in the hands of one person.[109] This wide definition provided in both the Regulation and CJEU jurisprudence means that significant amounts of data held in connected and autonomous vehicles is likely to be incorporated as personal data. For example, the European Commission notes that 'Data broadcast by C-ITS from vehicles will, in principle, qualify as personal data as it will relate to an identified or identifiable natural person.'[110] Moreover, the ICO noted that the collection of collision data, telematics, geolocation and driver settings would also be encompassed with personal data.[111]

Data usage

5.34 Article 6 of the GDPR states that in order for data to be processed lawfully, at least one of the six criteria within Article 6 must apply, including where 'the data subject has given consent'[112] or where 'processing is necessary for the performance of a contract to which the data subject is party or in order to take steps at the request of the data subject prior to entering into a contract'.[113] The requirement of data for contractual performance is likely to cause significant complexity for manufacturers, insurers and other parties. For example, as noted by the Federation Internationale de l'Automobile: 'In most cases monitoring of the vehicle and its components does not take place in the course of contract performance since a contractual relationship between OEM (manufacturer) and the customer does not necessarily exist.'[114] Moreover, even if a contract does exist, 'monitoring will not deemed to be a part of this contract, since product monitoring obligations qualify as public safety obligations'.[115]

106 (C-582/14) [2017] 1 WLR 1569.

107 The Court mentioned this in relation to the definition provided in 'Directive 95/46/EC of the European Parliament and of the Council of 24 October 1995 on the protection of individuals with regard to the processing of personal data and on the free movement of such data' (1995) *Official Journal of the European Union*, L 281, Article 2(a), which is similar to the definition provided in the GDPR particularly with regards to the term 'personal data'.

108 *Breyer* (n 105), [41].

109 Ibid., [43].

110 Communication from the Commission to the European Parliament, the Council, the European Economic and Social Committee and the Committee of the Regions, 'A European strategy on Cooperative Intelligent Transport Systems, a milestone towards cooperative, connected and automated mobility, Brussels, 30.11.2016 COM(2016) 766 final, 8.

111 Information Commissioner's Office (n 96), 1.

112 GDPR Article 6(1)(a).

113 GDPR Article 6(1)(b).

114 Federation Internationale de l'Automobile Region 1: Europe, The Middle East and Africa, 'What EU legislation says about car data: Legal Memorandum on connected vehicles and data' (2017), 18, www.fiaregion1.com/wp-content/uploads/2017/06/20170516-Legal-Memorandum-on-Personal-Data-in-Connected-Vehicles-www.pdf, accessed 31 August 2018.

115 Ibid.

5.35 Further, the GDPR has seemingly strengthened requirements in terms of consent, with Article 7(2) stating that the request for consent 'shall be presented in a manner which is clearly distinguishable from the other matters, in an intelligible and easily accessible form, using clear and plain language' and further providing in Article 7(3) that the data subject 'shall have the right to withdraw his or her consent at any time'. There will undoubtedly be significant difficulty for manufacturers and providers in relation to obtaining consent from data subjects due to greater awareness of individuals in relation to potential data misuse.

Data protection by design

5.36 Article 25 GDPR is based upon 'data protection by design or default' whereby companies are encouraged to implement technical or organisational measures during the design stage and throughout the lifecycle of the system.[116] The data controller must further implement mechanisms to ensure that only the personal data necessary for each specific purpose of the processing is processed.[117] Further, data which is held should not be made accessible to an indefinite number of persons without an individual's intervention.[118]

Post-Brexit

5.37 The UK has, by implementing the GDPR within the Data Protection Act 2018, shown its desire to ensure compatibility with EU regulation. However, even with the UK currently complying with the GDPR as it currently stands, there are complications, for example, concerning the future compatible interpretation of this regulation, as the UK will not be able to refer cases to the Court of Justice of the European Union.[119]

5.38 Moreover, with the likelihood that the UK will leave the European Economic Area and therefore become a third country, the European Commission will have to determine whether the UK's data protection laws meet the criteria contained in Article 45 GDPR. Under Article 45 GDPR, in order for the transfer of personal data to take place in relation to a third country, the Commission must confirm that there is an adequate level of data protection in that country.

116 Information Commissioner's Office, 'Data protection by design and default', https://ico.org.uk/for-organisations/guide-to-the-general-data-protection-regulation-gdpr/accountability-and-governance/data-protection-by-design-and-default, accessed 29 August 2018.

117 GDPR Article 25(2).

118 Ibid.

119 For discussion on the UK securing an adequacy decision, see Aysem Diker Vanberg and Maelya Maunick 'Data protection in the UK post-Brexit: the only certainty is uncertainty' (2018) *International Review of Law, Computers & Technology*, Vol. 32, No. 1, 190–206,194.

5.39 The UK is looking to go further than this, however, with a 'legally-binding data protection agreement'[120] between the EU and the UK, which the UK argued would give 'legal certainty and stability that an adequacy decision would not'.[121] The acceptance by the EU of such an agreement is not certain and will depend on negotiations.

Data access

5.40 There is clearly a significant theme emerging from the above in terms of 'personal data' protection, with much current legislation coming from within the EU. However, this does not significantly address the issue with regard to the access of personal data.

5.41 Cooperation and regulation at an international level is required as this is an issue that transcends borders. The UK DfT response to the House of Lords Science and Technology Committee noted, with an emphasis on some of the challenges that are being faced:

> The international debate on what data needs to be collected (beyond who, or what, was in control of the automated vehicle) still needs to take place. We need detailed engagement on who will need access to it, or how it should be shared to balance the needs of industry, the police and justice systems, and the privacy of vehicle users.[122]

5.42 The EU has also been focussing on the issue of data access and collection. The Gear 2030 group noted that 'the European Commission would need to consider how to ensure an effective stakeholder dialogue on issues related to data',[123] which is 'underpinned by the industry and service providers guaranteeing fair access, storage and sharing of vehicle data'.[124] The European Parliament has called on the Commission to 'publish a legislative proposal on access to in-vehicle data and resources by the end of the year'.[125] The Commission noted its position 'on the possibility for consumer to have access to different services, safety, cybersecurity, in full compliance with the legislation on competition and on the protection of personal data such as user consent for data sharing',[126] and is currently monitoring the situation.[127]

---

120 *Technical Note: Benefits of a New Data Protection Agreement* (HM Government, 2018), https://assets.publishing.service.gov.uk/government/uploads/system/uploads/attachment_data/file/714677/Data_Protection_Technical_Note.pdf, accessed 30 August 2018.

121 Ibid.

122 Department for Transport and Department for Business, Energy, Innovation and Skills, 'Response to House of Lords Science and Technology Select Committee report "Connected and Autonomous Vehicles: The future?" 2nd Report of Session 2016–17' (2017), www.parliament.uk/documents/lords-committees/science-technology/autonomous-vehicles/HMG-response-connected-autonomous-vehicles-report.pdf, accessed 29 August 2018.

123 GEAR 2030 High Level Group on the Competitiveness and Sustainable Growth of the Automotive Industry in the European Union, Final Report (2017), 32.

124 Ibid.

125 European Parliament, Motion for a European Parliament Resolution on a European strategy on Cooperative Intelligent Transport Systems (2017/2067(INI)), [41].

126 Communication from the Commission to the European Parliament, the Council, the European Economic and Social Committee, the Committee of the Regions 'On the road to automated mobility: An EU strategy for mobility of the future' Brussels, 17.5.2018 COM(2018) 283 final, 12–13.

127 Ibid., 13.

5.43 Significant discussion has already taken place at EU level in terms of 'guiding principles' for in-vehicle data access. The C-ITS Working Group 6[128] introduced five principles which should apply to data access: (1) Consent, (2) Fair and undistorted competition, (3) Data privacy and data protection, (4) Tamper-proof access and liability, and (5) Data economy. These 'guiding principles' evidently have the support of UK manufacturers.[129] The difficulty in meeting every principle in its entirety is evident. For example, the European Commission noted that technical proposals by Working Group 6 for the storage of in-car data, involving the On-board Application Platform, the In-vehicle Interface, and Data Server Platform, would not satisfy all 'guiding principles'.[130]

5.44 Finally, in relation to non-personal data, a regulation on 'a framework for the free flow of non-personal data in the European Union'[131] has already been proposed by the European Commission. This regulation would not be intended to be a set of detailed technical rules, but rather 'a clear, comprehensive and predictable legal framework for storage or other processing of data other than personal data in the internal market'.[132] It would provide that:

> Location of data for storage or other processing within the Union shall not be restricted to the territory of a specific Member State, and storage or other processing in any other Member State shall not be prohibited or restricted, unless it is justified on grounds of public security.[133]

Moreover, a single point of contact would be required in each Member State to ensure the application of the regulation.[134]

5.45 Over the course of 2018, there has evidently been a substantial push by organisations in the UK for data access to be regulated. Much of this concerned the need for UNECE regulation in relation to a 'Data Storage System for Automatically Commanded Steering Function'.[135] Questions will nevertheless revolve around the part to play of current and future EU regulation of data access and control, particularly post-Brexit.

128 C-ITS Working Group 6, 'Access to in-vehicle resources and data' (December 2015), 7. https://ec.europa.eu/transport/sites/transport/files/facts-fundings/tenders/doc/specifications/2015/s248-450626-annex6-report.pdf, accessed 31 August 2018.

129 Society of Motor Manufacturers and Traders, 'Connected and Autonomous Vehicles: Position Paper' (February 2017), www.smmt.co.uk/wp-content/uploads/sites/2/SMMT-CAV-position-paper-final.pdf, accessed 31 August 2018.

130 European Commission, 'Access to In-vehicle Data and Resources', Final Report (2017), 8, https://ec.europa.eu/transport/sites/transport/files/2017-05-access-to-in-vehicle-data-and-resources.pdf, accessed 29 August 2018.

131 Proposal for a Regulation of the European Parliament and of the Council on a framework for the free flow of non-personal data in the European Union Brussels, 13.9.2017 COM(2017) 495 final 2017/0228.

132 Ibid., Recital 7.

133 Ibid., Article 4.

134 Ibid., Article 7.

135 See para 3.31 in which this is discussed.

CHAPTER 6

International comparisons

Kyriaki Noussia

Introduction

6.1 Progress in automated driving can hardly be clearly distinguished from advances in other areas of technology. This includes areas such as robotics and autonomics, sensor technology and advances in information and communication technologies. Conclusions drawn from legal analyses and assessments in these fields can therefore be applied *mutatis mutandis* to the problems of autonomous vehicles and their driving. The central characteristics of the impending transformation in road transport, which entails that the latter will become part of the Internet of Things (IoT),[1] dictate the need to research, examine, discuss and analyse the way in which different jurisdictions have regulated or plan to regulate autonomous vehicles and their operation through the current or future enactment of legislation, in an effort to detect common patterns in regulation and ways to better tackle the arising issues. Hence, this chapter discusses the laws in place or in preparation for autonomous vehicles and automated driving as well as, wherever the gathered research material allows us, the transformation and impact of autonomous vehicles regulation on motor insurance in the various jurisdictions, the various cyber risks and the new technologies issues in relation to autonomous vehicles. The jurisdictions researched, discussed and analysed are Greece, Germany, Austria, Italy, the US and South Africa.

Greece

6.2 In the Greek legal system, there are no specific legal provisions regulating autonomous vehicles.[2] In relation to liability in tort from the use of autonomous vehicles, the relevant provisions applying with regard to autonomous vehicles and liability in tort from their use are derived from other

1 E. Hilgendorf, 'Automated Driving and the Law', in E. Hilgendorf and U.Siedel (eds), *Robotics, Autonomics and the Law, Robotik und Recht, Legal Issues Arising from the Autonomics for Industry 4.0 Technology Programme of the German Federal Ministry for Economic Affairs and Energy*, Vol. 14 (Nomos, 2017), 171–193, 171, 174–175.

2 Based on the answers provided by the Hellenic/Greek National Chapter to the AIDA Questionnaire on New Technologies, to be used in a report to be presented by the author of this chapter at the New Technologies Plenary Session at the XV AIDA World Congress in Rio, Brazil (October 2018).

laws – that is, constitute general laws – and are the provisions of (a) the Civil Code, particularly the general provisions on tort (articles 914–938); (b) the Law 2251/1994[3] on consumer protection, particularly article 6 on the Liability of Producer for Product Defects (which transposed into Greek legislation the EU Directives on product liability 85/374/EEC as amended by the Directive 1999/34/EC on the approximation of the laws, regulations and administrative provisions of the Member States concerning liability for defective products), as well as article 5 on the sale of consumers goods and guarantees and article 7 on health and security of consumers; (c) the joint Ministerial Decision Z3–2810/2004 (Official Journal B 1885/2004) on the general security of products which transposed into Greek legislation the Directive 2001/95/EC of 3 December 2001 on general product safety; and (d) the compulsory motor liability insurance.

6.3 With regard to insurance, to date there is no specific piece of legislation enacted in the Greek legal system to regulate the insurance of autonomous vehicles. However, the provisions of the Law 489/76 on compulsory motor liability insurance,[4] as amended, should also apply to issues of autonomous vehicles. The Law was codified by the PD no. 237/1986, and has been amended numerous times.[5] Greece has harmonised its motor insurance legislation with all EU Motor Insurance Directives. Particularly, Law 4364/2016 has harmonised the Law on compulsory motor liability insurance with the Fourth Motor Insurance Directive 2009/138/EC relating to insurance against civil liability in respect of the use of motor vehicles, and the enforcement of the obligation to insure against such liability.

6.4 According to article 1(a) of Law 489/76 as amended:[6]

> 'vehicle' means any vehicle intended for travel on land, but not running on rails, and propelled by mechanical or electrical power, regardless to the number of wheels. Vehicle also includes any trailer whether or not coupled behind the main vehicle, as well as a bicycle equipped with an auxiliary motor.

Also, according to article 2 of Law 489/76 as amended, 'an owner or holder of a vehicle which circulates on roads in Greece is obliged to have third-party liability insurance cover, in compliance with the Law'.

6.5 Since the definition of the term 'vehicle' is broad, it provides ground for a much broader interpretation with regard to its application. However, it will be a task for the courts to provide each time the relevant interpretation in each specific case, as a result of the use of these vehicles on the roads in

3 Which was amended by Law L. 3587/2007 (laws will be referred to as L. in footnotes).

4 The law entered into force on 1 January 1978.

5 There have been numerous amendments of the law 489/1976, as follows: L 1569/1985, PD. 1019/1981 and 118/1985, L. 1867/1989, PD 264/1991, PD 314/1993, L. 2170/1993, L. 2367/1995, PD. 252/1996, L. 2496/1997, L. 2648/1998, L. 2741/1999, L. 2753/1999, L. 2837/2000, L. 2919/2001, PD. 10/2003, L. 3419/2005, L. 3557/2007, L. 3693/2008, L. 3746/2009, L. 3867/2010, L. 3904/2010, L. 4092/2012, L. 4141/2013, L. 4261/2014, L. 4364/2016, L. 4438/2016 and L. 4484/2017.

6 In free translation from the Greek.

Greece and of potential legal issues and disputes that may arise. Potentially, the legislator may also assess that certain amendments or clarifications of the definition might be needed. To date, the use of the listed types of vehicles in Greece is still very limited; hence the above definition of 'vehicle' would apply to the types of vehicles used so far in Greece.

Motor vehicle insurance

6.6 The future of motor insurance is undoubtedly connected to the new opportunities emerging from new technologies, such as automated vehicles, telematics applications, etc. Further development of new technologies and their use in Greece may in certain cases require new regulations, starting from the definition of autonomous vehicles, civil liability issues and of insurance regulations.

6.7 The technological revolution would require a new generation of insurance products and would entail also significant changes in existing insurance procedures. Underwriting and claims handling procedures should also be designed *ab initio* in accordance with any arising new conditions. The main issue would be to clarify whether in the event of an accident the damage would be covered by the motor liability insurance and/or the product liability insurance legislation.[7]

6.8 It is anticipated that autonomous vehicles could potentially lead to a substantial reduction in motor insurance claims due to the expected reduction of motor accidents. Lower claims could result in lower premiums and tighter profit margins. The role of claims analysts and loss adjusters could also change due to the expected availability of significant data on the frequency and nature of accidents.

6.9 At present, few insurance companies in Greece have begun designing and offering new MTPL products based on telematics (e.g. black box technology GPS) which enables the insurer to track the driving record and behaviour of the insured in order to determine both the risk and liability entailed. At present, insurers using telematics devices in Greece incur the cost of their installation. As sensors and computers become more commonplace in vehicles, telematics-based policies will be increased.

Cyber risks

6.10 Under Greek law, the main pieces of legislation relevant to cyber risk are:

- Directive 95/46/EC of the European Parliament and of the Council of 24 October 1995 on the protection of individuals with regard to the processing of personal data and on the free movement of such data, which was transposed to the Greek legal order by Law 2472/1997;

7 Based on the answers provided by the Hellenic/Greek National Chapter to the AIDA Questionnaire on New Technologies, to be used in a report to be presented by the author of this chapter at the New Technologies Plenary Session at the XV AIDA World Congress in Rio, Brazil (October 2018).

- Regulation (EU) 2016/679 of the European Parliament and of the Council of 27 April 2016 on the protection of natural persons with regard to the processing of personal data and on the free movement of such data, repealing Directive 95/46/EC (General Data Protection Regulation), which applies as of 25 May 2018;
- Directive 2002/58/EC of the European Parliament and of the Council of 12 July 2002 concerning the processing of personal data and the protection of privacy in the electronic communications sector (Directive on privacy and electronic communications), which was transposed into Greek legislation by Law 3471/2006,[8] whereas the amendments to the Directive – that is, Directive 2006/24/EC of 15 March 2006 on the retention of data generated or processed in connection with the provision of publicly available electronic communications services or of public communications networks and amending Directive 2002/58/EC – were transposed by Law 3917/2011;[9]
- NIS Directive, Directive (EU) 2016/1148 of the European Parliament and of the Council of 6 July 2016 concerning measures for a high common level of security of network and information systems across the Union. The Member States should have adopted laws and regulations to comply with this Directive by 9 May 2018 and should have started its application from 10 May 2018.

6.11 Greece is currently in the process of preparing a cyber security strategy in compliance with the above EU legislation.

6.12 Property policies in the Greek insurance market exclude losses from cyber risks[10] and cyber risks insurance is mainly offered as a stand-alone insurance product.[11]

New technologies

6.13 New technologies are affecting the way in which insurance policies are placed. Direct business/sales channels (mainly internet-based) offer a direct link to the end customer, reduce significantly issuance time and offer to the company customer data for coverage-premium and behavioural analysis.

---

8 L. 3471/2006 Protection of personal data and private life in the electronic communication sector and amendments of L. 2472/1997.

9 L. 3917/2011 on the retention of data generated or processed in connection with the provision of publicly available electronic communications services or of public communications networks, use of surveillance systems by taking or recording audio or video in public places and other relevant provisions.

10 They cover material/physical damage (e.g. property software) to the property arising out of covered perils (e.g. fire, lightning, explosion, etc.), but exclude any loss, damage, destruction, distortion, erasure, corruption or alteration of data from any cause (including computer virus, computer malicious acts/computer malware/human error system failure on insured's computer systems, cyber extortion, etc.).

11 But in some cases general liability policies (professional indemnity policies) and property policies may include a cyber extension.

Additionally, the use of portals and services by sales agents to place/issue policies results in more efficient delivery of the end product to the customer and the use of technologies by customers and sales agents (i.e. website, mobile applications, etc.) reduces the company's administrative costs. New technologies are also applied to the agents' and brokers' training (e.g. e-learning).

6.14 The means of providing information to policyholders are already changing. Customers are directed to websites and mobile applications' personalised webpages, and are receiving emails and SMS texts regarding their policies. Traditional channels take advantage of new technologies to eliminate the time intervals and administrative costs. However, the use of new technologies has to follow the insurance legislation and therefore written documents have not been vastly replaced; according to the existing legislation, insurance policies should still be issued and sent to the insured in print.

Germany

6.15 The German Road Traffic Act (RTA; *Straßenverkehrsgesetz*, *StVG*) ensures that both the driver and the so-called keeper (*Halter*) – the registered holder of the car who decides on its use and who bears the running expenses, and who will often but not necessarily be its owner at the same time[12] – of a motor vehicle are liable for damages caused by the use of the vehicle.[13]

6.16 In 2017 the RTA was amended in order to include rules for automated driving. The liability of the driver is regulated in Section 18 RTA. According to that provision the driver has to compensate any third party for damages and financial losses that were negligently caused by the driver during the use of the vehicle on public roads. There is a legal presumption of negligence,[14] which, however, leaves the driver the possibility to prove that there was no negligence.[15] Section 7 RTA states that the keeper of a vehicle is liable for any damage inflicted in relation to its use, regardless of whether or not the keeper was driving the car. Hence, Section 7 RTA imposes a strict liability on the keeper, since liability does not require any kind of negligent action of the keeper or the driver.[16]

6.17 The liability system of the RTA is based on two pillars: fault-based liability of the driver with a presumption of negligence, and strict liability of the keeper.

6.18 The German legislator has addressed the need to alter the law to respond to the use of highly or fully automated vehicles on public roads, and on 21 June 2017 a number of new sections entered into force, in particular

12 *Bundesgerichtshof* (*BGH*) (10 July 2007) in [2007] Neue Juristische Wochenschrift (NJW), 3120 marginal no. 7; this section is produced based on the answers provided by the German National Chapter (Prof. Ch. Armbruster of the Freie Universitaet Berlin) to the AIDA Questionnaire on New Technologies, to be used in a report to be presented by the author of this chapter at the New Technologies Plenary Session at the XV AIDA World Congress in Rio, Brazil (October 2018).

13 Section 7 para 1, 18 para 1 RTA.

14 Section 18 para 1 section 2 RTA.

15 Section 12 para 1 nos 1 and 2 RTA.

16 *Bundesgerichtshof* (*BGH*) (26 April 2005) in [2005] Neue Juristische Wochenschrift (NJW), 2081 et seq.

a new Section 1a and 1b of the RTA. Section 1a RTA states that highly or fully automatized vehicles may be used on public roads under the condition that the automated functions are working properly. The legislator left the above-mentioned liability system essentially unchanged.[17]

6.19 Section 1a para 2 RTA only defines which vehicles are categorized as highly or fully automated in the sense of the wording of the RTA – that is, a vehicle that has technical equipment which can control the respective motor vehicle after activation in order to cope with the driving task, including longitudinal and transverse guidance; which is able to comply with the traffic regulations relating to vehicle guidance during highly or fully automated vehicle control; which can be manually overridden or deactivated at any time by the vehicle operator; which can detect the necessity of the vehicle's own control by the vehicle driver; which can indicate visually, acoustically, tactilely or otherwise perceptibly to the vehicle operator the requirement of the vehicle control unit with sufficient time before the vehicle control is handed over to the driver; which refers the driver to a use contrary to the system description.

6.20 The car manufacturers are obliged to explicitly confirm the compliance of their vehicles with the above-mentioned requirements in the system description.[18] Furthermore, the legislator has expressly pointed out that the use of one or more driver assistance systems leaves the classification of the person enabling these systems as driver of the vehicle unaffected.[19]

6.21 The amendments of the RTA establish some important obligations of the driver when using driver assistance systems in a highly or fully automated vehicle. According to Section 1b RTA, the driver is not allowed to turn his attention completely away from the traffic. This means that the driver must not rely entirely on the automated driving system. In the event that the driver notices or has to notice because of obvious circumstances that the preconditions for use of the highly or fully automated mode are no longer met, he is obliged to take back control over the car. The same applies where the vehicle itself advises the driver to switch off the assistance system.[20] Taking into account the fact that the danger automated cars bring cannot yet be fully estimated, the legislator decided to double the maximum liability for personal damage from €5 million to €10 million.[21] The RTA does not impose any special obligations on the keeper of the vehicle when he allows third parties to use the highly or fully automated vehicle. As the general principles of Section 7 RTA prevail, the keeper is still responsible for any damage caused by the use of the highly or fully automated vehicle.

17 Ch. Armbrüster, *Automatisiertes Fahren – Paradigmenwechsel im Straßenverkehrsrecht, Zeitschrift für Rechtspolitik* (ZRP), 2017, pp. 83 et seq.

18 Section 1a para 2 RTA.

19 This section is produced based on the answers provided by the German National Chapter (Prof. Ch. Armbruster of the Freie Universitaet Berlin) to the AIDA Questionnaire on New Technologies, to be used in a report to be presented by the author of this chapter at the New Technologies Plenary Session at the XV AIDA World Congress in Rio, Brazil (October 2018).

20 Section 1b para 2 RTA.

21 Section 12 para 1

6.22 If an accident solely resulted from the malfunction of a driver assistance system, the keeper of the car may be able to take recourse against its producer. Currently, there are no specific rules for product liability with regard to highly or fully automated vehicles, and as per the Product Liability Act (Section 1 para 1, PLA; *Produkthaftungsgesetz*, *ProdHaftG*), which transposed the EU Product Liability Directive[22] into German law, when a defective product causes a person's death, bodily injury or damage to health, or damage to property, the producer has to compensate the damage. Under certain circumstances, however, which have to be proven by the producer, he will escape strict liability.[23]

Motor vehicle insurance

6.23 In accordance with the relevant EU directives, German law requires the keeper of a car to obtain liability insurance cover (Section 1 Compulsory Insurance Act [CIA, *Pflichtversicherungsgesetz*, *PflVG*]). This also applies to highly or fully automated vehicles. The insurance cover has to include damage caused by an unauthorized driver. Furthermore, the CIA establishes minimum standards with regard to the insurance sum and the obligations the insurance contract may contain. Clauses that deviate from the compulsory provisions are void. In contrast, other car-related insurance contracts – that is, property insurance that covers damage suffered by the policyholder himself in the event of an accident – are not mandatory under EU or German law. In practice, however, car insurance products combining third-party liability insurance and property insurance are often sold in Germany.

6.24 It is estimated that the increasing use of digitalisation in vehicles will augment the relevance of product liability insurance but will not diminish the role of motor insurance.[24, 25]

Cyber risks

6.25 In June 2015 the German legislator enacted the IT Security Act (*IT-Sicherheitsgesetz*), which mainly aims to improve the IT security of companies.

22 Directive 85/374/EEC.

23 E.g. the liability of a producer is excluded if the state of scientific and technical knowledge at the time when the product was put into circulation was not such as to enable the defect to be discovered; this section is produced based on the answers provided by the German National Chapter (Prof. Ch. Armbruster of the Freie Universitaet Berlin) to the AIDA Questionnaire on New Technologies, to be used in a report to be presented by the author of this chapter at the New Technologies Plenary Session at the XV AIDA World Congress in Rio, Brazil (October 2018).

24 J. Müller, 'Wie das autonome Fahren die Kfz-Versicherung verändern wird', www.allianzdeutschland.de/wie-das-autonome-fahren-die-kfz-versicherung-veraendern-wird/id_79691618/index, accessed 4 October 2018.

25 This section is produced based on the answers provided by the German National Chapter (Prof. Ch. Armbruster of the Freie Universitaet Berlin) to the AIDA Questionnaire on New Technologies, to be used in a report to be presented by the author of this chapter at the New Technologies Plenary Session at the XV AIDA World Congress in Rio, Brazil (October 2018).

6.26 As per Section 8a para 1 of the Federal Office for Information Security (*Bundesamt für Sicherheit in der Informationstechnik, BSI*) Act, operators of critical infrastructure must provide reasonable organisational and technical precautions to prevent disruption of the availability, integrity, authenticity and confidentiality of their information technology systems, components or processes.

6.27 In addition to the development of a high IT security level, members of critical infrastructures are obliged to notify security breaches to the BSI (Section 8b para 4 BSI Act). In order to meet legislative targets, the IT Security Act strengthens the position of the BSI, particularly by extending duties and powers. Moreover, the German legislator and the competent administrative authorities have enacted further specific rules on cyber security in different acts.[26]

6.28 In July 2016, the EU Directive on Security of Network and Information Systems (NIS Directive) passed the European Parliament.[27]

6.29 Both EU and German Data Protection laws contain IT security requirements to protect personal data, but not with a particular focus on cyber threats. Part B Sections 32 to 34 EU General Data Protection Regulation (*Datenschutzgrundverordnung, DSGVO*) draw up provisions regarding security of personal data.[28]

6.30 Many forms of damage relating to cyber risks are already covered by standard indemnity and property insurance policies.[29] The German Insurance Industry Association (*Gesamtverband der deutschen Versicherungswirtschaft, GDV*) has developed specific model terms and conditions of cyber risk insurance,[30] which have been published as non-binding recommendations for the industry. This cyber risk insurance covers financial losses caused by an information security breach.[31]

New technologies

6.31 New technologies are not often mentioned in the German Federal Constitution (GG), at least as far as the actual wording is concerned. The right to conduct research (article 5(3) GG) includes the right to develop new vehicle technologies. As per the jurisprudence of the German Constitutional Court (*Bundesverfassungsgericht*), fundamental rights form an objective value

26 Section 109 Telecommunication Act (*TKG*); Section 13 Telemedia Act (*TMG*): Section 25a Banking Act (*KWG*); Section 33 Securities Trading Act (*WpHG*); Section 44 Atomic Energy Act (*AtomG*); Section 11 Energy Industry Act (*EnWG*).

27 TaylorWessing, 'The German IT Security Law – Fact Sheet', https://deutschland.taylorwessing.com/de/the-german-it-security-law-fact-sheet, accessed 4 October 2018.

28 Section 83 EU General Data Protection Regulation.

29 Lexology, 'PRA demands action on silent cyber risk', www.lexology.com/library/detail.aspx?g=54176adb-7f80-43cf-8552-a5a63e018c72, accessed 4 October 2018.

30 General terms and conditions of cyber risk insurance (T&Cs Cyber) provided by the GDV, www.versicherungskurier.de/id/4853490/Cyber-Versicherung-GDV-praesentiert-Musterbedingung, accessed 18 October 2018.

31 This section is produced based on the answers provided by the German National Chapter (Prof. Ch. Armbruster of the Freie Universitaet Berlin) to the AIDA Questionnaire on New Technologies, to be used in a report to be presented by the author of this chapter at the New Technologies Plenary Session at the XV AIDA World Congress in Rio, Brazil (October 2018).

system aiding in interpretation but also containing obligations for the state. The state is obliged to protect the physical integrity and lives of its citizens and as such has the obligation to promote such technologies that contribute to the protection of constitutionally protected legal rights or interests.

6.32 Freedom of movement on the road enjoys constitutional protection as a fundamental right and automated vehicles do not hinder this right, especially since their introduction is being done on a step-by-step basis.[32]

6.33 New technologies have already begun to disrupt the traditional distribution of insurance products by agents and brokers. The effects and influences of new technologies on the traditional use of agents and brokers are immense and of a vast variety. Broker applications (apps), which have flooded the German distribution sector in recent years, have triggered much controversy and brought up a number of legal issues.[33] In general, those applications are frequently structured as a kind of 'digital insurance folder', which allows not only the conclusion of new contracts through the application, but also the digitalisation of existing policies. These new technologies business models therefore significantly depend on the IT infrastructure of the individual insurance company.

6.34 A key issue with broker applications is the proper transmission of information to the customers. Big data models and analysis methods, as well as new data sources, have enabled insurers and distributors to gather information concerning individual risk on a large scale. Any processing of personal data[34] needs to be justified either by consent or by statutory provision.[35] Special provisions apply to so-called special categories of data.[36]

6.35 Furthermore, data protection law limits big data analysis methods and the required gathering of large amounts of data, stating that personal data shall be adequate, relevant and limited to what is necessary in relation to the purposes for which they are processed (principle of data minimisation).[37]

6.36 The gathering of enormous amounts of personal data solely for the purpose of accidentally finding links between them is forbidden under EU and

---

32 E. Hilgendorf, 'Automated Driving and The Law', in E. Hilgendorf and U.Siedel (eds), *Robotics, Autonomics and the Law, Robotik und Recht, Legal Issues Arising From The AUTONOMICS for Industry 4.0 Technology Programme of the German Federal Ministry for Economic Affairs and Energy*, Vol. 14 (Nomos, 2017), 171–193, 176–177.

33 Ch. Armbrüster and S. Pfeiffer, *Rechtsfragen rund um Versicherungs-Apps*, Zeitschrift für Versicherungswesen (ZfV), 2016, pp. 277 et seq.

34 Personal data is defined as any information relating to an identified or identifiable natural person ('data subject'); an identifiable natural person is one who can be identified, directly or indirectly, in particular by reference to an identifier such as a name, an identification number, location data, an online identifier or to one or more factors specific to the physical, physiological, genetic, mental, economic, cultural or social identity of that natural person (Art. 4 para 1 GDPR).

35 Art. 83 para 5 GDPR.

36 If the personal data processed are classified as such special categories of personal data (such as data revealing racial or ethnic origin, political opinions, religious or philosophical beliefs, or trade union membership, and genetic data, biometric data, data concerning health or data concerning a natural person's sex life or sexual orientation) (Art. 9 GDPR), the permissiveness of processing such data for the purpose of risk assessment – at least in the ordinary course of events – depends on the consent of the data subject (applicant).

37 Art. 5 para 1 lit. c

German data protection law. In addition, even when big data analysis methods comply with the principle of data minimisation, the aggregation of data for the purposes of profiling is further limited and restricted by Article 22 of the EU General Data Protection Regulation (GDPR).[38] German law does not prohibit the transmission of pre-contractual information via the internet. The only requirement that must be met is that all pre-contractual information has to be communicated to the customer on a durable medium.[39, 40]

Austria

6.37 Laws on autonomous vehicles in Austria include the new automated driving ordinance (Ordinance of the Federal Ministry of Transport, Innovation and Technology on the Framework for Automated Driving), which stipulates the prerequisites for the testing of vehicles with assistance systems as well as vehicles with automated or connected drive systems entered force on 19 December 2016; however, such systems are still not allowed to be operated in the normal course of traffic.

6.38 Before each test drive the responsible ministry of transport must, *inter alia*, be provided with the following information:

- information on the application or system being tested;
- name of the testing facility;
- the total number of real, virtual and experimentally driven test kilometres completed by the system being tested;
- licence plate number for the test vehicle to be used in test runs;
- information on the test vehicle driver for the test runs;
- written confirmation from the motor vehicle liability insurer that insurance coverage is provided for the test runs in accordance with the provisions of the Motor Vehicle Liability Insurance Act 1994.

6.39 A legal obligation to obtain a motor vehicle liability insurance exists. Such insurance provides coverage for claims with respect to property, personal or any other pecuniary damages due to traffic accidents caused by the vehicle. The amount of the insurance coverage is dependent on the horsepower and the age of the vehicle. A confirmation regarding the existence of motor vehicle liability insurance must be provided to the Ministry of Transport prior to the first entry service of the vehicle.

6.40 According to Section 1(3), para 1 of the above-mentioned ordinance, the testing of vehicles in public traffic is only allowed where during the test drive(s) insurance coverage is guaranteed by a liability insurer and where the motor vehicle

38 Regulation (EU) 2016/679.

39 Section 7 para. 1 sent. 1, 61 para 1 VVG and Art. 25 IDD.

40 This section is produced based on the answers provided by the German National Chapter (Prof. Ch. Armbruster of the Freie Universitaet Berlin) to the AIDA Questionnaire on New Technologies, to be used in a report to be presented by the author of this chapter at the New Technologies Plenary Session at the XV AIDA World Congress in Rio, Brazil (October 2018).

liability insurer confirms in writing that insurance coverage, in accordance with the provisions of the Motor Vehicle Liability Insurance Act 1994 (KHVG 1994), is provided for the applied test drive(s).

Motor vehicle insurance

6.41 With respect to the future of motor vehicle insurance as this will be changed or reshaped due to autonomous vehicles, there are currently no actions and/or initiatives being taken by the insurance industry. The use of 'big data' is already commonplace in Austria and used to improve the claim settlement and optimise the classification of the car and its potential risk (e.g. theft risk).

Cyber risks

6.42 Several paragraphs were added to the Austrian Criminal Code:

- unlawful access to a computer system (paragraph 118a);
- abusive/unlawful interception of data (paragraph 119a);
- data corruption (paragraph 126a);
- disruption of the functioning of computer systems (paragraph 126b);
- abuse of access data (paragraph 126c).

6.43 Cyber risks are generally excluded from coverage. Only a specific cyber insurance is providing self-damage coverage (business interruption loss, crisis management, extortion costs, data restoration costs, credit monitoring costs, defence costs, forensic costs, notification costs, public relations costs, contractual penalties of PCI companies) and liability coverage. Although there are currently 11 different products offered on the market, it must be emphasised that the provided coverage of said products can differ significantly. Most insurance concepts or products do not cover risks associated with the use of cloud services, cyber terrorism, operating errors and financial loss because of cyber fraud. In addition, deductibles are always part of the existing insurance concepts/products and several insurers are stipulating sub limits for individual insurance components (e.g. credit monitoring costs, contractual penalties of PCI companies).

New technologies

6.44 Brokers are maintaining online presences, however, mainly by focusing on client information. Nevertheless, different online brokers have entered the marketplace and are currently facing the challenge to comply with their legal obligations to provide advice to their clients according to the local broker law and as a result they are frequently sued by their competitors under the Austrian federal act against unfair competition.

6.45 Big data is especially relevant in the area of motor vehicle insurances (e.g. regarding risk classification or computation of replacement value). In principle, all Austrian insurers maintain online portals. Those portals enable insurers to offer direct sales on their online portals. Some portals also provide additional features such as online damage tracking (e.g. Zurich Connect). Such online portals are not only designed for direct insurance customers; in addition, brokers are usually also directed to those portals for insurance applications/calculations. In short, it is obvious that most insurance companies are emphasising the improvement of their online presence. In spite of this digital trend, certain elements, such as policy documents, are still submitted to the policy holder by post, although it has been permitted by law since 2012 to provide such documents electronically.

6.46 The risks to critical infrastructure (electricity supply, water supply, public transport, hospitals, airports, banks) were recognised and hence the EU issued in 2016 the Directive (EU) 2016/1148 of the European Parliament and of the Council of 6 July 2016 (the NIS Directive) concerning measures for a high common level of security of network and information systems across the Union.[41]

Italy

6.47 Vehicles are primarily regulated at the state level by way of Legislative Decree No. 285/1992, as modified ('Traffic Code'). Legislative Decree No. 422/1997 provides Italian regions and provinces with the authority to identify specific rules in relation to public transport. Italy has not issued any regulation specifically related to driverless vehicles. However, on 12 February 2014, the Italian Ministry for Infrastructures and Transportation issued the National Plan of Action for the Smart Systems of Transportation with the aim to promote improvement in the regulatory, organisational, technological and financial conditions within the sector of intelligent transportation systems (ITS). This plan, however, does not specifically take into account autonomous vehicles.[42]

6.48 Current laws do not permit autonomous vehicles to use public roads unless a human driver has proper control of the vehicle. However, in theory, states and territories have road traffic exemption powers to allow testing of autonomous vehicles on public roads, even if these tests would more likely take place on tracks closed to the general public.

6.49 Also, according to Presidential Decree No. 474/2001, which regulates tests on the use of vehicles on roads, the obligation to have a vehicle registration and a licence plate does not apply when the Ministry for Infrastructures and Transportation issues a specific authorisation for the vehicle to be used in roads, for technical, experimental or manufacturing tests.

6.50 In general terms, vehicles (including autonomous vehicles) have to meet the standards set out in the applicable EU Directives and Regulations

41 This section is produced based on the answers provided by the Austrian National Chapter to the AIDA Questionnaire on New Technologies, to be used in a report to be presented by the author of this chapter at the New Technologies Plenary Session at the XV AIDA World Congress in Rio, Brazil (October 2018).

42 Baker McKenzie, Global Driverless Vehicle Survey 2018, 112–118, 112. www.bakermckenzie.com/-/media/files/insight/publications/2018/03/global-driverless-vehicle-survey-2018/mm_global_driverlessvehiclesurvey2018_mar2018.pdf, accesed 18 October 2018.

and the Traffic Code. Having said that, due to the lack of a specific regulation on autonomous vehicles, in order for the latter to be used or tested, they must successfully undergo an approval process. Such a process is likely to take several months, in order to obtain authorisation from both the ministerial and local administrative levels.[43]

6.51 No specific laws or law proposals exist in relation to liability in tort for injuries inflicted by the use of autonomous vehicles and vessels, and there is no law specifically relating to compulsory insurance coverage for injuries inflicted by the use of autonomous vehicles. However, the use of motor vehicle will certainly change in the coming years in terms of insurance requirements. It will be necessary to cover the risks to property and the product liability, and not the responsibility of the owner/driver.[44]

6.52 Given the lack of a specific regulation concerning autonomous vehicles, the general rules on the use of vehicles on roads apply, as set forth in Section 2054 of the Italian Civil Code. Pursuant to this provision, the driver is liable for any damages caused by the use of the vehicle on roads, unless the driver is able to prove that he/she has done everything he/she could to prevent any damage. Moreover, if a car accident happens, all drivers involved in the accident are deemed jointly responsible for having caused the damage, unless proven otherwise.

6.53 It will be interesting to see how courts, through case law, will interpret the above-mentioned rule, considering that autonomous cars would not have a driver inside the car who can be held liable for the accident. In this respect, it will certainly be necessary to provide autonomous cars with technological systems that help establish whether the autonomous car is liable in any way for the accident. In the affirmative, depending on the cause of the accident (e.g. an inherent defect of the car or an error in programming the route by the owner), the manufacturer or the owner could be held liable. In this respect, pursuant to Section 1.184 of Law No. 124/2017, the Italian government will also have to issue, in 2018, one or more legislative decrees aimed at regulating the installation on vehicles of the so- called 'black boxes' or other similar electronic systems, in order to create technological platforms for an integrated urban development scheme.[45]

Cyber risks

6.54 In Italy there are, at the moment, no specific laws on cyber risks. In relation to cyber risks, insurance policies cover three types of damages – that is, direct and indirect material and immaterial damages as well as for insurance for legal expenses and legal assistance.

43 Baker McKenzie, Global Driverless Vehicle Survey 2018, 129. www.bakermckenzie.com/-/media/files/insight/publications/2018/03/global-driverless-vehicle-survey-2018/mm_global_driverlessvehiclesurvey2018_mar2018.pdf, accessed 18 October 2018.

44 This section is produced based on the answers provided by the Italian National Chapter to the AIDA Questionnaire on New Technologies, to be used in a report to be presented by the author of this chapter at the New Technologies Plenary Session at the XV AIDA World Congress in Rio, Brazil (October 2018).

45 Baker McKenzie, Global Driverless Vehicle Survey 2018, 112–118, 114.

New technologies

6.55 In Italy, new technologies already affect the placement of insurance policies via the use of roboadvisors and the use of social media in brokerage. New technologies also affect underwriting and will reshape it. Insurance companies use big data to create an algorithm able to check a client, the object of the insurance and the risk. Insurance companies have a new role, not preventing risk or informing people about risks, but influencing the habits of the clients. In this way the risks are reduced and not just checked. This phenomenon is called 'InsurTech' and it allows companies to understand the needs of clients and accordingly indicate the best product to cover the risks involved. But this phenomenon has the disadvantage of cyber risks for the client's privacy. The means of providing information to policy holders depends and has to comply with the Italian Insurance Regulator's (IVASS) Regulation 8/2015 which serves the purpose of simplifying contractual relationships between insurance companies, intermediaries and clients, using technological, electronic and web systems. Both the Italian insurance companies and the intermediaries are obliged to have a certified email, and they have to indicate this in all their correspondence and on their website. They have to sign the insurance policies with an electronic signature; if this is done, then the policies could be in electronic form. Insurance companies and intermediaries need also to observe the various laws on privacy and to have in place online and free payment systems. It is essential that prior to the conclusion of the contract the insurer and the intermediaries receive from the prospective insured the consent to send the related insurance documents via the internet at a specific pre-contractual or contractual moment. Consent can be given with regard to a specific, current or future contract.

6.56 New technologies have also affected the insurance industry in Italy in that 'green cars' gain a reduction of the motor insurance premium and also in that in Italy some insurance companies offer eco-driving policies as well as providing systems to evaluate the eco-driving habits of their customers in order to determine annual premiums. It is possible to control eco-driving habits through a black box installed in the car and through car inspection via various techniques. Hence, such techniques are registered by black boxes which can control and influence eco-driving habits; however, these entail potential issues regarding the protection of the privacy of the driver and of the occupants. At the moment, the use of black boxes is generally permitted only for a reconstruction of an accident dynamic.[46]

46 This section is produced based on the answers provided by the Italian National Chapter to the AIDA Questionnaire on New Technologies, to be used in a report to be presented by the author of this chapter at the New Technologies Plenary Session at the XV AIDA World Congress in Rio, Brazil (October 2018).

USA

6.57 In the USA, federal law does not yet expressly regulate autonomous vehicles. However, both the House of Representatives and the Senate have proposed legislation to regulate certain aspects of highly automated vehicles.

6.58 On 6 September 2017, the House of Representatives passed the Safely Ensuring Lives Future Deployment and Research in Vehicle Evolution Act ('SELF DRIVE Act'), which regulates certain aspects of autonomous vehicles and expressly pre-empts state laws that conflict with performance and design standards of autonomous vehicles set by the federal government. On 28 September 2017, the Senate introduced the American Vision for Safer Transportation through Advancement of Revolutionary Technologies Act ('AV START Act'), which also regulates certain aspects of autonomous vehicles and expressly pre-empts state laws that conflict with performance and design standards of autonomous vehicles set by the federal government.[47] On 12 September 2017, the Trump Administration released a new policy document titled 'Automated Driving Systems 2.0: A Vision for Safety' updating the Federal Automated Vehicle Policy which replaced the document that had been released by the National Highway Traffic Safety Administration (NHTSA) in September 2016.[48]

6.59 Prior to that, the National Highway Traffic Safety Administration (NHTSA) had released its Preliminary Statement of Policy Concerning Automated Vehicles on 30 May 2013. On 14 January 2016, US Transportation Secretary Anthony Foxx announced the President's fiscal year 2017 budget proposal and policy guidance which updates the Preliminary Statement. The update was issued in September 2016. On 4 February 2016, the NHTSA responded to a request from Google, Inc. to interpret several provisions in the Federal Motor Vehicle Safety Standards as they apply to the described design for vehicles that Google is developing and testing. On 20 September 2016, the US Department of Transportation issued its federal policy for automated vehicles.[49]

6.60 The 2016 NHTSA policy update had four parts: vehicle performance guidelines, model state policy, the NHTSA's current regulatory tools and possible new regulatory actions which the NHTSA believed could be helpful in ensuring the safe deployment of autonomous vehicles. For potential autonomous vehicle manufacturers, the policy included a set of 15 best practices regarding the safe pre-deployment design as well as development and testing of autonomous vehicles prior to commercial sale or operation on public roads.

47 To become law, however, the House of Representatives and the Senate must reconcile the proposed bills and the President must sign the final legislation.

48 NHTSA, 'Automated Driving Systems: A Vision for Safety', www.nhtsa.gov/sites/nhtsa.dot.gov/files/documents/13069a-ads2.0_090617_v9a_tag.pdf, accessed 4 October 2018.

49 The Center for Internet and Society, 'Automated Driving: Legislative and Regulatory Action', http://cyberlaw.stanford.edu/wiki/index.php/Automated_Driving:_Legislative_and_Regulatory_Action, accessed 4 October 2018.

6.61 The four US states of California, District of Columbia, Florida and Nevada were amongst the first to have passed laws allowing and setting the conditions for the testing of automated and highly autonomous vehicles. In addition, the USA has often been cited as having dealt foremost with the issue of legalising autonomous cars. In June 2011, the Nevada legislature passed a law to authorise the use of autonomous cars, thus becoming the first jurisdiction in the world where autonomous vehicles could be legally operated on public roads.[50]

6.62 To date, however, 21 states and the District of Columbia have enacted laws related to autonomous vehicles: Alabama, Arkansas, California, Colorado, Connecticut, Florida, Georgia, Illinois, Louisiana, Michigan, Nevada, New York, North Carolina, North Dakota, Pennsylvania, South Carolina, Tennessee, Texas, Utah, Virginia and Vermont. State laws generally (i) legalise the deployment and operation of highly automated vehicles in their jurisdiction (e.g. Colorado), (ii) create a framework for testing highly automated vehicles (e.g. New York), (iii) authorise platooning of highly automated vehicles (e.g. South Carolina), or (iv) merely create committees tasked with conducting studies related to driverless vehicles (e.g. Alabama). In other states, such as Arizona, executive orders have been issued by the state governor permitting the testing of highly automated vehicles (rather than by enacting new laws through the state legislature).[51]

6.63 September 2016 was a turning point in terms of the state legislature as well: California transportation authorities made two major changes in their policy on autonomous vehicles. The first change, a new bill signed into law, gives the Contra Costa Transportation Authority permission to test a pilot project on public roads without having a driver behind the wheel. Prior to this, the state only allowed public road testing if a human driver was in the driver's seat and capable of taking immediate manual control of the vehicle in the event of an autonomous technology failure or other emergency. The bill requires the autonomous vehicles to be insured for $5 million, for the self-driving automobiles to not exceed 35 miles per hour on the road, and for testing data to be shared with the government and whilst placing geographic restrictions. Testing can only take place at two locations: at a former Concord Naval Weapons Station and current AV testing facility, and at the San Ramon Bishop Ranch office park. The second change, the revised draft regulations which were released by California's department of motor vehicles, can potentially change how all autonomous vehicles are tested in the state by rolling out the privileges given to the aforementioned pilot programme. If the law passes (it is still under legislative procedure), it will allow car manufacturers to test vehicles deemed safe by the federal government on public roads without licensed drivers. Instead of having a driver in the vehicle, the newly

50 Nowadays, most of the US states deal with the basic legal status of autonomous vehicles.
51 Baker McKenzie, Global Driverless Vehicle Survey 2018, 229–241, 229–230.

proposed regulations require that a test driver has two-way communication with a vehicle.[52]

6.64 On 12 September 2017, the Secretary of Transportation released an updated policy that overrides the Federal Automated Vehicles Policy previously released in September 2016. The 2017 Guidance ('Automated Driving Systems 2.0: A Vision for Safety') clarified that the NHTSA is not contemplating a new regulatory regime specific to autonomous vehicles. The NHTSA will instead use its current regulatory powers, such as enforcing compliance with federal performance and design standards, in order to regulate autonomous vehicles. The 2017 Guidance also reaffirmed that safety assessment letters are purely voluntary – that is, an entity does not need to submit a safety assessment letter to NHTSA prior to testing its driverless vehicle in the USA.

6.65 Importantly, the 2017 Guidance may conflict with certain provisions of the SELF DRIVE Act, which reference the 2016 version of the NHTSA Federal Automated Vehicles Policy. For instance, safety assessment letters are voluntary under the 2017 Guidance, but would become mandatory if the SELF DRIVE Act is signed into law in its current form. In addition, the 2017 Guidance strongly encourages states to refrain from enacting performance and design standards applicable to autonomous vehicles. Under the SELF DRIVE Act, such standards would be expressly pre-empted by federal law to the extent that a conflict exists between the federal and state-level standard.[53]

6.66 On 6 September 2017, the House of Representatives passed the SELF DRIVE Act. The SELF DRIVE Act creates significant responsibilities for the United States Department of Transportation (USDOT) with respect to regulation of autonomous vehicles, automated driving systems and components of automated driving systems. If enacted, the most significant feature to manufacturers will be the dramatic increase in exemptions that NHTSA may grant to entities for the purpose of testing autonomous vehicles. The USDOT will be required to create a publicly available electronic database of vehicles exempt from federally mandated design and performance standards.

6.67 Pursuant to the SELF DRIVE Act, the Secretary of Transportation will develop a safety assessment certification process that requires entities developing autonomous vehicles to address the safety of their respective driverless vehicles, including fail-safe features. Prior to promulgation of this safety assessment certification process, entities will be required to submit safety assessment letters as contemplated by the 2016 version of the Federal Automated Vehicles Policy. The Secretary of Transportation must also develop a safety priority plan that will identify components of autonomous vehicles that may require performance

52 'California Revises Draft Regulations for Autonomous Vehicles', www.omm.com/resources/alerts-and-publications/alerts/california-revises-draft-regulations-for-autonomous-vehicles, accessed 4 October 2018; V. Ilková and A. Ilka (2017) 'Legal Aspects of Autonomous Vehicles – an Overview'. Proceedings of the 21st International Conference on Process Control (PC), Štrbské Pleso, Slovakia, 6–9 June 2017, pp. 428–433, 430.

53 Baker McKenzie, Global Driverless Vehicle Survey 2018, 229–241, 240.

standards, including human machine interfaces, sensors and actuators, and headlamps. Pursuant to the safety priority plan, NHTSA is responsible for identifying 'procedure standards' related to software and cyber security in driverless vehicles.[54]

6.68 The SELF DRIVE Act prohibits manufacturers from selling any highly automated vehicle unless the manufacturer has developed a privacy plan that includes descriptions of certain practices regarding the collection, use, sharing and storage of information about vehicle owners or occupants. The SELF DRIVE Act provides the Federal Trade Commission with enforcement authority. To promote uniformity, the SELF DRIVE Act federally preempts any state or local laws that conflict with federal laws related to motor vehicle safety standards, design, construction and performance of driverless vehicles. The SELF DRIVE Act also requires the Secretary of Transportation to create a methodology for describing the capabilities of autonomous vehicles or partially automated vehicles for the purpose of informing consumers. Manufacturers will be required to inform consumers of their respective autonomous vehicles' capabilities in accordance with the methodology.

6.69 On 28 September 2017, the Senate introduced the AV START Act, which also regulates certain aspects of highly automated vehicles and expressly pre-empts state laws that conflict with performance and design standards of autonomous vehicles set by the federal government. The AV START Act requires the Department of Transportation to issue a report that identifies conflicts with respect to existing federal motor vehicle safety standards and the use and testing of highly automated vehicles and proposals to resolve such conflicts. The AV START Act requires each manufacturer introducing a highly automated vehicle or automated driving system into interstate commerce to provide a safety evaluation report to the Secretary of Transportation. The safety evaluation report shall include information concerning system safety, data recording, cyber security, human–machine interface, crashworthiness, capabilities and limitations, post-crash behaviour, the account of applicable traffic laws, and automation function performance. Such reports will be made publicly available, but manufacturers may submit trade secret or confidential information separately from the report.

6.70 To engage the industry, the AV START Act requires the Secretary of Transportation to establish a Highly Automated Vehicles Technical Committee to provide a forum for stakeholders to discuss, prioritise and make technical recommendations for highly automated vehicles and automated driving system safety. The Committee may also establish various working groups with industry representatives. Significantly, the AV START Act requires manufacturers of highly automated vehicles and automated driving systems to create cyber security plans, which must meet the requirements of the AV START Act, and must be submitted to the Secretary of Transportation for inspection.

54 Baker McKenzie, Global Driverless Vehicle Survey 2018, 229–241, 237–239.

To promote uniformity, the AV START Act also federally pre-empts any state or local laws that conflict with federal laws related to motor vehicle safety standards, design, construction and performance of driverless vehicles.

6.71 In relation to liability in tort from the use of autonomous vehicles, under Colorado law liability for a crash involving an autonomous vehicle is determined in accordance with applicable state, federal or common law. However, there is no uniformity across the states regarding liability in the event of a collision. Some states might provide that the vehicle owner is liable, other states might provide that the person who engaged the autonomous vehicle driving system is liable, whereas other states might provide that autonomous vehicle driving system itself is liable.[55]

New technologies

6.72 Autonomous vehicles hold the promise of saving tens of thousands of lives each year in the USA, and many more worldwide, reducing traffic, saving energy and providing mobility to those who cannot drive conventional cars. Nonetheless, autonomous vehicles will inevitably have some accidents. On balance, autonomous vehicles are likely to prevent many more accidents than they cause, but there will be at least some accidents involving autonomous vehicles that would not have occurred with conventional vehicles.

6.73 Because of accidents involving autonomous vehicles, some of which may be catastrophic, product liability litigation is inevitable, especially in cases where conventional vehicles would not have crashed. The threat of massive product liability litigation involving autonomous vehicles is widely perceived as one of the chief obstacles to their development and sales, if not the number-one threat. Some believe that product liability suits are an existential threat to autonomous driving. Crippling suits could force manufacturers to exit the market and may deter some manufacturers from entering the market because of a belief that the sales are not worth the risk. If these dire predictions come to pass, the USA and other parts of the world experiencing a flood of lawsuits may lose the use of a technology that would save many times more lives than it would endanger. If, however, the industry finds effective ways to manage the risk of product liability, it can bring to the market a lifesaving technology whilst maintaining practices to minimise accidents and resulting liability, as well as the profitability needed to offer autonomous vehicles in the market over time.[56]

6.74 We do not yet know with certainty from practice what kinds of alleged defects will likely result in litigation. Nonetheless, the history of automotive litigation, discussions with those in the industry and judgments about what is likely to come all suggest that there will be many sources of potential defects that may give rise to product liability litigation. Autonomous vehicles

55 Baker McKenzie, Global Driverless Vehicle Survey 2018, 229–241, 236.

56 S.S. Wu, 'Product Liability Issues in the U.S. and Associated Risk Management', in M. Maurer et al. (eds), *Autonomous Driving*, Springer, 2016, 553–569, 553–554.

will share some of these sources of defects with conventional vehicles, but some of them will be unique to autonomous vehicles. The most interesting and perhaps most concerning potential defects will be those in the software used for autonomous driving.

6.75 Defendants may assert a number of defences against a product liability case. The most common types of defences relate to the conduct of the plaintiff. In some cases, the defendant contends that the plaintiff's negligent conduct caused or contributed to an accident. The viability of a defence, based on a plaintiff's own negligence, depends on state law and the type of claim, but a defendant may also use it as evidence of a superseding cause of an accident. In addition, some accidents occur because a plaintiff misused or modified a product. Finally, a plaintiff may not be able to recover all damages if he or she failed in some way to mitigate the damages. Many of these defences may have limited application to persons driving autonomous vehicles in autonomous mode. If the plaintiff was not in control of the vehicle at the time of the accident, the plaintiff could not have driven carelessly. Once autonomous vehicles enter the mass market, a seller cannot realistically contend that the plaintiff assumed the risk of driving a vehicle using new and untested technology. Nonetheless, it is likely over time that some people will modify their autonomous vehicles or try to abuse the sensors or control systems for fun. In these cases, if an accident occurs, the defendant may point to this conduct as a defence. The other key defence in autonomous vehicle litigation will likely be a 'state of the art' defence to a design defect claim. The basis of this defence is that the manufacturer could not have produced a safer design at the time of sale because safer designs were not technologically feasible then. Such a defence is valid in some states but not in others.

6.76 Manufacturers should manage the risk of autonomous vehicles' liability, which in its turn can enable them to make safer products that are less likely to cause litigation-triggering accidents: by planning ahead; by considering the commitment they make to product safety using a proactive approach which would entail not just meeting minimum standards; by conducting careful risk analysis on all issues in the design of autonomous vehicles; by obtaining insurance coverage to manage product liability risk and hence shift the risk of product liability to insurance carriers; by working together on industry risk management initiatives; by deploying effective records and information management skills.[57]

6.77 Lawsuits in which manufacturers appear callous, placing profits over safety, face the risk of huge liabilities. Overall, the threat of crippling product liability litigation in the USA poses a profound concern for manufacturers of autonomous vehicles, but starting proactive engineering design strategies for safety risk management and legal strategies to anticipate future litigation now can place manufacturers in the best position to maximise product safety and minimise product liability in upcoming decades.

57 S.S. Wu, 'Product Liability Issues in the U.S. and Associated Risk Management', in M. Maurer et al. (eds), *Autonomous Driving* (Springer, 2016), 553–569, 560–568.

South Africa

6.78 There is no law or regulations related to autonomous vehicles. Autonomous vehicles will fall under the meaning of 'motor vehicle' under the National Road Traffic Act (NRTA), and the provisions applicable to motor vehicles under the NRTA will also apply to autonomous vehicles.

6.79 Motor vehicles are primarily regulated by national legislation that is binding on all nine provinces of South Africa, the salient of which are:

- the National Road Traffic Act, No. 93 of 1996 (NRTA);
- the Road Accident Fund Act, No. 56 of 1996 (RAF Act); and
- the National Regulator for Compulsory Specifications Act, No. 5 of 2008 (NRCSA).

6.80 The NRTA regulates, *inter alia*, (i) the registration and licensing of motor vehicles; (ii) the fitness of drivers and licensing of human beings to operate (drive) motor vehicles; (iii) the fitness of vehicles, road safety, transportation of dangerous goods; (iv) road traffic signs and general speed limits; (v) accidents and reports; and (vi) reckless and negligent driving.

6.81 The NRCSA provides the Compulsory Specifications with which every motor vehicle that is to be registered and licensed in terms of the NRTA has to comply. The RAF Act provides for compensation to a third party for damage (limited to bodily injuries) or loss caused by or arising from the driving of a motor vehicle.

6.82 South African law does not provide for any general liability specifically linked to driverless cars. The following applies in respect to the issue of liability when motor vehicles are in involved in collisions.

6.83 The RAF Act provides for a state-mandated insurance fund for the compensation of third-party damages, which are limited to bodily injuries, or loss caused by or arising from the driving of a motor vehicle. The regime put in place by the RAF Act is premised on income derived from a fuel levy that is to be applied to the Road Accident Fund (RAF), which primarily goes to the compensation of road accident victims. This is achieved by the RAF finding the wrongdoer in the motor vehicle accident – that is, one who would have ordinarily been civilly liable under South African common law. The definition of 'motor vehicle' in the RAF Act appears to be broad enough to encompass a driverless vehicle. The relevant wrongdoer would be either the person who activated the driverless system or the one who failed to take control of the vehicle when he or she ought to have done so.

6.84 With regard to damage caused by or arising from the driving of a motor vehicle that is *not* related to bodily injury (i.e. patrimonial loss related to, for instance, the motor vehicle itself), the general principles of the law of delict (i.e. tort law) will be applied as between the 'driver' of the autonomous vehicle and the driver of the other motor vehicle with outcomes being heavily dependent on the facts and circumstances of the collision.[58]

58 Baker McKenzie, Global Driverless Vehicle Survey 2018, 169–176, 171–172.

Critical comparative assessment

6.85 Under the Greek legal system, there are no specific legal provisions regulating autonomous vehicles. Likewise, liability in tort from the use of autonomous vehicles is regulated via the provisions of other general laws. Insurance of autonomous vehicles is also not specifically regulated to date and the provisions of Law 489/76 on compulsory motor liability insurance, as amended, applies. The definition of the term 'vehicle' is broad and allows the inclusion of its application to autonomous vehicle; however, it remains to be interpreted by the courts.

6.86 The use of autonomous vehicles could potentially lead to a substantial reduction in motor insurance claims and hence lower premiums. The main pieces of legislation relevant to cyber risk under Greek law are the EU Directives/Regulations on data protection, security of network and information systems. Greece is preparing a cyber security strategy in compliance with the above EU legislation. As property policies in the Greek insurance market exclude losses from cyber risks, such coverage is mainly offered as a stand-alone insurance product. New technologies are affecting the way in which insurance policies are placed and the means of providing information to policyholders are changing already.

6.87 In Germany, the 2017 amendment of the RTA included rules for automated driving. The liability of the driver dictates the compensation of any third party for damages and financial losses that were negligently caused by the driver during the use of the vehicle on public roads. Liability is also strict on the keeper of the vehicle as no negligent action is required. Hence the RTA introduces fault-based liability of the driver – with a presumption of negligence – and strict liability of the keeper. The amendments of the RTA establish obligations of the driver when using driver assistance systems in a highly or fully automated vehicle. It does not impose any special obligations on the keeper of the vehicle when he allows third parties to use the highly or fully automated vehicle. Damages relating to cyber risks are already covered by standard indemnity and property insurance policies

6.88 In Austria a new automated driving ordinance stipulates the prerequisites for the testing of autonomous vehicles. 'Big data' is used in Austria to improve the claim settlement and optimise the classification of the car and its potential risk. Cyber risks are generally excluded from coverage.

6.89 In Italy, autonomous vehicles are regulated via the laws regulating ordinary vehicles. There are no specific laws or law proposals in relation to liability in tort for injuries inflicted by the use of autonomous vehicles and the general rules of the Italian Civil Code the use of vehicles on roads apply. Also no specific laws exist on cyber risks. New technologies are introduced via the use of roboadvisors and the use of social media in brokerage and the promotion and monitoring of eco/green cars and drivers.

6.90 In the USA there is federal and state regulation for autonomous vehicles. The SELF DRIVE Act and AV START Act regulate autonomous vehicles, and numerous states have, to date, enacted laws related to autonomous vehicles. As per the SELF DRIVE Act, the Secretary of Transportation will develop a safety assessment certification process for autonomous vehicles. The Act imposes the obligation to have a plan on data security and protection.

6.91 In relation to liability in tort from the use of autonomous vehicles, there is no uniformity across the states regarding liability in the event of a collision.

6.92 In South Africa, there is no special law or regulation related to autonomous vehicles and the law provides compensation to a third party for damage (limited to bodily injuries) or loss caused by or arising from the driving of a motor vehicle.

6.93 From the jurisdictions examined, we notice a disparity in the enactment or not of laws for the regulation of autonomous vehicles. Some countries have enacted special laws on autonomous vehicles regulation and others have not. When no special law exists, general motor legislation and liability in tort apply. Cyber risks are excluded and provided as separate insurance cover. However, in Germany, damages relating to cyber risks are already covered by indemnity and property policies. The jurisdictions examined also include laws which provide for compensation to a third party for damage or loss by the driving of an autonomous vehicle.

Conclusions

6.94 The harmonisation, at international level, of laws relating to the regulation of autonomous vehicles should be of high priority and significance. Our discussion has revealed similar or different patterns in the way various legal systems have regulated, in relation to autonomous vehicles, via the enactment of legislation or plan to do so. As demonstrated by our discussion, it appears essential to have homogenous law through legal harmonisation at international level.

6.95 Until this happens, it is also essential to allow the development of mechanisms for autonomous vehicles to be able to adapt/switch software packages when the automated vehicle crosses national borders. As long as the law applicable to the driver and driving are different from country to country (and it is impossible to predict how long this will be the case), the on-board computer must be programmed so that it is able, upon crossing a border, to apply the relevant rules of the country where the car is located at that moment in time. An example of this would be the accident prevention algorithm, as per which the software containing the driving rules would need to be exchanged or occur automatically at the point where the border was crossed. The legal issues associated with this, from simple civil liability issues to questions of international law, still have to be clearly identified, let alone be resolved. Hence, the need to examine comparative legal regimes and legislations for autonomous vehicles and seek the promotion of harmonisation of laws at international level in the years to come.[59]

59 E. Hilgendorf, 'Automated Driving and the Law', in E. Hilgendorf and U. Siedel (eds), *Robotics, Autonomics and the Law, Robotik und Recht, Legal Issues Arising from the AUTONOMICS for Industry 4.0 Technology Programme of the German Federal Ministry for Economic Affairs and Energy*, Vol. 14 (Nomos, 2017), 171–193, 191–193.

CHAPTER 7

Future developments

Matthew Channon, Lucy McCormick and Kyriaki Noussia

Overview

7.1 As discussed in previous chapters, the UK's legal and regulatory system is already one of the most welcoming for the development of autonomous vehicle technology. The intention is for the UK to remain at the forefront through a 'rolling programme of reform that will keep our regulations up to date, ensuring we can safely take advantage of what automated vehicles can offer, tailored to near-to-market technologies'.[1] The first fruit of this programme was the Automated and Electric Vehicles Act 2018.[2] The government has also issued several pieces of non-statutory guidance, notably the 'The Pathway to Driverless Cars: A Code of Practice for testing'[3] and 'The key principles of vehicle cyber security for connected and automated vehicles'.[4]

7.2 Most recently, in March 2018, the government announced the start of a three-year project by the Law Commission of England and Wales and the Scottish Law Commission to undertake a far-reaching review of the UK's legal framework for road-based autonomous vehicles. The Commissions will be considering a wide variety of areas of law, ranging from road traffic legislation to product liability. They will also look at the use of autonomous vehicles as part of modern public transport networks and on-demand passenger services.[5] The first year of the project is intended to include an audit of the current law and a scoping exercise to identify key issues. The full report is anticipated to be released in March 2021.[6]

7.3 There are certainly a number of areas which are ripe for reform in the near future, notably aspects of the Road Vehicle (Construction and Use)

1 'Pathways to Driverless Cars: Proposals to support advanced driver assistance systems and automated vehicle technologies' (Centre for Connected and Autonomous Vehicles, 2016), Foreword, https://assets.publishing.service.gov.uk/government/uploads/system/uploads/attachment_data/file/536365/driverless-cars-proposals-for-adas-and_avts.pdf, accessed 31 August 2018.

2 See Chapter 3.

3 See Chapter 2.

4 See Chapter 5.

5 The project will not cover drones or vehicles designed solely for use on pavements. It will also not address data protection and privacy, theft and cyber security, or land use policy.

6 For more information on the Law Commission's project, see Law Commission, 'Automated Vehicles', www.lawcom.gov.uk/project/automated-vehicles, accessed 28 August 2018.

Regulations 1986 and of the Highway Code. Looking further forward, we may also see more radical changes to the regimes for insurance, civil and criminal liability, the driving test, the MOT and so on. These possibilities are discussed below.

The near future

The Road Vehicle (Construction and Use) Regulations 1986

7.4 The government is considering changes to the Road Vehicle (Construction and Use) Regulations 1986 to accommodate emerging technologies, notably remote-control parking.

7.5 Most relevant to remote-control parking are Regulations 104, 107 and 110. Some changes have already been made. Regulation 110 was amended in June 2018 by the Road Vehicles (Construction and Use) (Amendment) Regulations 2018/592 Regulation 2(2) to accommodate the use of remote-control parking technologies. Regulation 110 prohibits the use of hand-held mobile communication devices while driving, subject to limited exceptions for emergencies. The June 2018 amendment added an additional paragraph 5(A) to make clear that using a mobile device while outside the vehicle to perform a remote-control parking function was permissible:

> (5A) A person does not contravene a provision of this regulation if, at the time of the alleged contravention—
>
> (a) that person is using the mobile telephone or other device only to perform a remote controlled parking function of the motor vehicle; and
> (b) that mobile telephone or other device only enables the motor vehicle to move where the following conditions are satisfied—
>   (i) there is continuous activation of the remote control application of the telephone or device by the driver;
>   (ii) the signal between the motor vehicle and the telephone or the motor vehicle and the device, as appropriate, is maintained; and
>   (iii) the distance between the motor vehicle and the telephone or the motor vehicle and the device, as appropriate, is not more than 6 metres.[7]

7.6 As to Regulations 104 and 107, these have not yet been amended but may well be in the near future. The former provides that 'No person shall drive or cause or permit any other person to drive, a motor vehicle on a road if he is in such a position that he cannot have proper control of the vehicle or have a full view of the road and traffic ahead.' There is arguably some uncertainty as to how this would be applied in a remote-control parking context. This could readily be

7 These features reflect some of the requirements found in the United Nations Regulation No. 79 (Regulation ECE 79.02), which came into force on 10 October 2017. Regulation ECE 79.02 updates the international type approval standard for steering equipment, which introduces, for the first time, requirements for a remote-control parking function. Regulation ECE 79.02 is made under the Agreement of the United Nations Economic Commission for Europe 1958 (Revision 3) ('UNECE 1958 Agreement').

clarified by adding a statement that a driver meets this requirement even if he is not in the driving seat, as long as he has the ability to control the vehicle through a hand-held device. Similarly, Regulation 107 requires that a driver must switch off the engine when not attending a vehicle. This could be clarified by adding a statement that an individual, though not in the driving seat, is deemed to be attending the vehicle when they are driving it, or are about to drive it, using a hand-held device.[8]

7.7 Also relevant to autonomous technologies generally is Regulation 109, which provides that the driver must not be in a position to see (directly or by reflection) a television set or similar screen showing moving images, in order to prevent driver distraction. This is subject to exceptions which are related to the driving task, such as fuel levels, speed, satellite navigation, reversing cameras and so on. As automated technologies become more advanced to the stage where the driver need not pay attention to the driving task, it is possible that this regulation could be relaxed to allow the driver to watch advertising, films and so on. However, at present this is some way away.

The Highway Code

7.8 Similarly, there are a number of respects in which the Highway Code[9] is beginning to fall behind emerging technology. The Department for Transport has consulted on amendments to the Highway Code rules 149, 150, 160 and 239.[10] Such amendments will provide more detailed provision as to how features such as remote-control parking and motorway assist technologies can be safely used. It is planned for such amendments to the Highway Code to be made in coordination with a wider series of amendments to the Highway Code in spring 2019.[11]

---

8 'Pathway to driverless cars: Consultation on proposals to support advanced driver assistance systems and automated vehicles – Government Response' (Centre for Connected and Autonomous Vehicles, 2017), 3.17–3.29, https://assets.publishing.service.gov.uk/government/uploads/system/uploads/attachment_data/file/581577/pathway-to-driverless-cars-consultation-response.pdf, accessed 31 August 2018.

9 The Highway Code is non-statutory but is relevant to legal liability. See Section 28(7) of the Road Traffic Act 1988 to the effect that 'A failure on the part of a person to observe a provision of the Highway Code shall not of itself render that person liable to criminal proceedings of any kind but any such failure may in any proceedings (whether civil or criminal, and including proceedings for an offence under the Traffic Acts, the Public Passenger Vehicles Act 1981 or sections 18 to 23 of the Transport Act 1985) be relied upon by any party to the proceedings as tending to establish or negative any liability which is in question in those proceedings'. See also *Wakeling v McDonagh* [2007] EWHC 1201, [24] (QB) in which Judge Mackie QC held that 'Any breach of the Highway Code is relevant but not determinative', and *Goad v Butcher* [2011] EWCA Civ 158, [9] in which Moore-Bick LJ held: 'A failure to observe the Highway Code might be evidence of negligence causing or contributing to a road traffic accident, but whether it was would depend very much on the circumstances in which the question was committed and who the claimant was.'

10 To align with the amendment which was made to Regulation 110 of the Road Vehicle (Construction and Use) Regulations 1986 in June 2018. See para 7.4 above.

11 Explanatory Memorandum to the Road Vehicles (Construction and Use) (Amendment) 2018 2018 No. 592.

7.9 Currently, the Highway Code provides at Rule 149 that:

> You MUST exercise proper control of your vehicle at all times. You MUST NOT use a hand-held mobile phone, or similar device, when driving or when supervising a learner driver, except to call 999 or 112 in a genuine emergency when it is unsafe or impractical to stop. Never use a hand-held microphone when driving. Using hands-free equipment is also likely to distract your attention from the road. It is far safer not to use any telephone while you are driving or riding – find a safe place to stop first or use the voicemail facility and listen to messages later.

7.10 It is anticipated that the government will amend this to accommodate remote-control parking, by adding a sentence to make clear that 'You can park your vehicle via remote control, using a legally compliant parking application or device in an appropriate way which does not endanger others'.[12]

7.11 Similarly, the Highway Code currently provides at Rule 150 that:

> There is a danger of driver distraction being caused by in-vehicle systems such as satellite navigation systems, congestion warning systems, PCs, multi-media, etc. You MUST exercise proper control of your vehicle at all times. Do not rely on driver assistance systems such as cruise control or lane departure warnings. They are available to assist but you should not reduce your concentration levels. Do not be distracted by maps or screen-based information (such as navigation or vehicle management systems) while driving or riding. If necessary find a safe place to stop.

7.12 It is anticipated that the government will update this by replacing the reference to 'cruise control or lane departure warnings' with a wider reference to 'motorway assist, lane departure warnings, or remote control parking', and by adding a sentence to make clear that 'If you are using advanced driver assistance systems, like motorway assist, or a remote control parking application or device, then you as the driver are still responsible for the vehicle and MUST exercise full control over these systems at all times'.[13] This is with a view to emphasising responsible use of such systems. As the technology evolves further and becomes sufficiently advanced that it does not require driver monitoring, it is possible that more substantially revised wording would be brought in.[14]

7.13 As to Rule 160, this currently provides, *inter alia*, that 'once moving you should…drive with both hands on the wheel where possible. This will help you to remain in full control of the vehicle at all times.' Drivers

---

12 'Remote Control Parking and Motorway Assist: Proposals for Amending Regulations and the Highway Code' (Centre for Connected and Autonomous Vehicles, December 2017), 1.32–1.33, https://assets.publishing.service.gov.uk/government/uploads/system/uploads/attachment_data/file/669442/remote-control-parking-motorway-assist-proposals-for-amending-regulation-and-highway-code.pdf, accessed 29 August 2018.

13 'Remote Control Parking and Motorway Assist: Proposals for Amending Regulations and the Highway Code' (Centre for Connected and Autonomous Vehicles, December 2017), 1.34–1.36, https://assets.publishing.service.gov.uk/government/uploads/system/uploads/attachment_data/file/669442/remote-control-parking-motorway-assist-proposals-for-amending-regulation-and-highway-code.pdf, accessed 29 August 2018.

14 'Pathways to Driverless Cars: Proposals to support advanced driver assistance systems and automated vehicle technologies' (Centre for Connected and Autonomous Vehicles, 2016), 3.3–3.5.

are increasingly using technologies which facilitate releasing their hold on the steering wheel for short periods, such as automated parking. Accordingly, it is anticipated that the government will add an additional sentence to make plain that 'You may use advanced driver assistance systems, if used in accordance with the manufacturer's or developer's instructions'.[15]

7.14 Finally, the government is also anticipated to amend Rule 239, which sets out the driving behaviours expected of someone when parking their vehicle. It is proposed to amend this by adding additional wording dealing with remote-controlled parking as follows:

> If you are using a handheld device to carry out a parking manoeuvre, then you must ensure that it is safe to do so before beginning the manoeuvre and should try to carry out the manoeuvre in the shortest, safest route possible. When parking, as the driver you MUST remain in control of the vehicle at all times; you must not use the device for other functions or in such a way that would cause danger to other road users. You should act in accordance with the manufacturer's or developer's instructions.[16]

7.15 Interestingly, the government does not currently plan to amend Rule 126, which provides that 'You must drive at a speed that will allow you to stop well within the distance you can see to be clear. You should allow at least a two-second gap between you and the vehicle in front on roads carrying faster moving traffic and in tunnels where visibility is reduced.' This provision is relevant to the possibility of 'platooning', namely the linking of two or more vehicles in convoy, using connectivity technology and automated driving support systems. These vehicles automatically maintain a set, close distance between each other and are able to accelerate or brake simultaneously. Platooning allows for a closer headway between vehicles by eliminating reacting distance needed for human reaction. The technology is anticipated to have substantial benefits, notably by way of vehicles in the slipstream using less fuel. To allow platooning to be a realistic commercial prospect in the UK, it would be necessary to relax Rule 126 to allow a shorter gap between vehicles. However, at present there is understood to be little public appetite for this.[17]

---

15 'Remote Control Parking and Motorway Assist: Proposals for Amending Regulations and the Highway Code' (Centre for Connected and Autonomous Vehicles, December 2017), 1.37–1.38, https://assets.publishing.service.gov.uk/government/uploads/system/uploads/attachment_data/file/669442/remote control-parking-motorway-assist-proposals-for-amending-regulation-and-highway-code.pdf, accessed 29 August 2018.

16 'Remote Control Parking and Motorway Assist: Proposals for Amending Regulations and the Highway Code' (Centre for Connected and Autonomous Vehicles, December 2017), 1.39–1.40, https://assets.publishing.service.gov.uk/government/uploads/system/uploads/attachment_data/file/669442/remote-control-parking-motorway-assist-proposals-for-amending-regulation-and-highway-code.pdf, accessed 29 August 2018.

17 Centre for Connected and Autonomous Vehicles, 'Pathway to Driverless Cars: Proposals to support advanced driver assistance systems and automated vehicle technologies' (July 2016) 3.26–3.30, https://assets.publishing.service.gov.uk/government/uploads/system/uploads/attachment_data/file/536365/driverless-cars-proposals-for-adas-and_avts.pdf, accessed 30 August 2018.

Looking further forward

Insurance

7.16 The Automated and Electric Vehicles Act 2018 (AEVA 2018) was only the first of a number of likely changes to the insurance over the coming years. For example, the role of the Motor Insurers' Bureau (MIB) in relation to uninsured or untraced vehicles will likely be a focus in the near future. In its 2016–2020 Strategic Review, the MIB noted the significant impact of autonomous vehicles on the insurance market and the MIB, although 'the fundamental changes that will flow from the widespread use of semi and fully autonomous vehicles are probably beyond the three to five year time horizon'.[18] The MIB's role is susceptible to significant change in the future, with questions in particular surrounding whether its role could be expanded to manage the retrieval of data for insurers.

7.17 There will also undoubtedly be further focus on the UK's anticipated departure from the European Union (Brexit), and its impact on the insurance of autonomous vehicles. The EU heavily regulates conventional motor insurance through the Sixth Consolidated Motor Insurance Directive (MID),[19] which equally applies to autonomous vehicles.[20] The impact of Brexit on the UK's compliance with these Directives is uncertain, and significant divergence between UK and EU rules may cause complexities regarding cross-border travel and coverage, including the end of the 'visiting victims' scheme. However, subject to European Commission approval, the UK government has already made the decision to keep the UK in the motor insurance 'Free Circulation Zone', meaning that vehicles could continue to travel across borders on their domestic policies and without the need for a green card.[21]

7.18 In an autonomous vehicles context, further complexity may surround significant differences with regard to legislation which has already been introduced and will likely be introduced in the future. The UK has already set out its insurance and liability framework clearly through the AEVA 2018, which, rather strangely in some circumstances, puts the UK more

18 Motor Insurers' Bureau, 'MIB – Strategic Review Future direction: 2016–2020' (2016), www.mib.org.uk/media/332294/issue-mibstrategicreview_futuredirection2016_2020highres.pdf, accessed 28 August 2018.

19 Directive 2009/103/EC of the European Parliament and of the Council relating to insurance against civil liability in respect of the use of motor vehicles, and the enforcement of the obligation to insure against such liability [2009]. OJ L 263.

20 See European Commission, 'Proposal for a Directive of the European Parliament and of the Council amending Directive 2009/103/EC of the European Parliament and the Council of 16 September 2009 relating to insurance against civil liability in respect of the use of motor vehicles, and the enforcement of the obligation to ensure against such liability' Brussels, 24.5.2018 COM (2018) 336 final 2018/0168 (COD), 7.

21 See Association of British Insurers, 'Drivers get the green light for hassle free post Brexit driving in the EU' (May 2018), www.abi.org.uk/news/news-articles/2018/05/drivers-get-the-green-light-for-hassle-free-post-brexit-driving-in-the-eu, accessed 28 August 2018.

in line with the Directives than some rules on conventional vehicles.[22] The MID provides, as noted by the European Parliament, a less harmonised framework for motor vehicles, due to not covering substantive rules on liability, which is where many of the compatibility issues could arise. In its own assessment,[23] one of the European Parliament's policy options, which it argued would be 'extremely difficult',[24] would be to encompass liability rules for autonomous vehicles within the Directive. Further questions surround the means of compensation under EU law of victims where the vehicle is hacked, since (as noted in the European Parliament) hacking is 'not an issue/risk explicitly or sufficiently clearly regulated by EU law'.[25]

7.19 Interestingly, the European Commission, in its recent proposal for a new MID,[26] proposed no changes to take into account the development of autonomous vehicles. This was on the basis that, for the purpose of the Directive, 'the absence of a driver is not relevant', and insurance is still required to cover for accidents involving autonomous vehicles.[27] The second step whereby insurers seek to recover from the manufacturer for product defect, according to the Commission, 'falls outside the scope of the Directive'.[28] This, it seems, follows the report from the Gear 2030 High Level Group which stated that insurance and liability rules are 'sufficient at this stage', at least for systems expected by 2020.[29] The group noted that the MID ensures a 'fast, simple and efficient means of compensation',[30] with the insurer then able to claim against the manufacturer for product defects under the Product Liability Directive.[31]

---

22 See, for example, the UK rules on exclusion clauses. The AEVA 2018 prohibits virtually all exclusion clauses to be used, which puts the UK in line with the Court of Justice of the European Union decisions in C-129/94 Criminal Proceedings against *Bernaldez* [1996] ECR I-1829 and C-409/11 *Csonka v Magyar Allam* [2014] 1 CMLR 14. Whereas for conventional vehicles as noted in *Bristol Alliance v Williams* [2012] EWCA Civ 1267, the UK legislative framework permits exclusions to be used.

23 European Parliament, 'A common EU approach to liability rules and insurance for connected and autonomous vehicles' (2018), www.europarl.europa.eu/RegData/etudes/STUD/2018/615635/EPRS_STU(2018)615635_EN.pdf, accessed 31 August 2018.

24 Ibid., 31.

25 Ibid., 21.

26 Proposal for a Directive of the European Parliament and of the Council amending Directive 2009/103/EC of the European Parliament and the Council of 16 September 2009 relating to insurance against civil liability in respect of the use of motor vehicles, and the enforcement of the obligation to ensure against such liability Brussels, 24.5.2018 COM(2018) 336 final 2018/0168 (COD).

27 Commission Staff Working Document Impact Assessment Accompanying the Document Proposal for a Directive of the European Parliament and of the Council amending Directive 2009/103/EC of the European Parliament and the Council of 16 September 2009 relating to insurance against civil liability in respect of the use of motor vehicles, and the enforcement of the obligation to insure against such liability {COM (2018) 336 final} - {SEC(2018) 248 final} - {SWD (2018) 248 final}, 19.

28 Ibid.

29 Gear 2030 High Level Group, 'The Report of the High Level Group on the Competitiveness and Sustainable Growth of the Automotive Industry in the European Union (GEAR 2030)' (2017), 44. The Gear 2030 group was formed by the European Commission in October 2015, bringing together Member States and key stakeholders.

30 Ibid., 44.

31 Council Directive 85/374/EEC concerning liability for defective products.

It seems therefore, for the time being, that there is no significant incompatibility between UK and EU law in this area. However, any departure of the UK in this area from the terms of the MID, or if the EU decides to harmonise liability or make a significant departure from its current regulatory approach to autonomous vehicles, could prompt significant challenges at a later stage.

7.20 Looking much further forward, it has been suggested that, ultimately, fully autonomous vehicles might be made exempt from the mandatory insurance requirements. The basis for this argument is that fully autonomous vehicles may eventually become so safe that collisions become almost unheard of.[32] The underlying rationale for requiring mandatory insurance for motor vehicles is that driving is a particularly hazardous activity; if driving became no more hazardous than walking down the street, why would specific insurance be necessary? While an interesting thought experiment, this prediction ignores the continuing prospect of autonomous vehicles being damaged through theft, arson, or hacking – or collision with other non-autonomous road users. As such, insurance is likely to continue to be mandatory for the foreseeable future.

Civil liability

7.21 There is currently no legislation specifically concerned with the liability for accidents involving autonomous vehicles. Parliament has legislated in relation to the insurance of automated vehicles, making insurers liable to pay in the first instance in certain circumstances, but that does not settle the underlying question of legal liability.[33] As discussed in Chapter 4, it is possible to make some predictions as to the likely liability position. Nonetheless, Parliament may decide to pass specific legislation dealing with liability in an autonomous vehicle context.

7.22 A particular area of possible development concerns product liability. The principal UK laws on product liability and safety are based on EU directives. If, as anticipated, the UK leaves the EU on 30 March 2019, in principle it becomes open to the UK to diverge from EU norms. The Product Liability Directive was implemented in the UK in the Consumer Protection Act 1987, and the latter has been widely considered a success and so is unlikely to be radically amended. Nonetheless, the CPA 1987 came into force before automated vehicles were a realistic prospect, and as such it is in certain respects a poor fit in relation to such technology.[34] It is possible that some minor changes could be made to the CPA 1987 – or a freestanding Act brought into being – which would make the UK product liability regime a better fit for autonomous vehicles.

32 According to the Royal Society for the Prevention of Accidents, 95% of all road accidents involve some human error, and in 76% of road accidents the human is solely to blame. Factors include alcohol, tiredness and impatience. Fully autonomous vehicles would not make these mistakes.

33 I.e. the Automated and Electric Vehicles Act 2018.

34 See para 4.7.

Criminal reform

7.23 There are a number of questions surrounding criminal liability for autonomous vehicle accidents. The most significant of these concerns whether it is would be the manufacturer or driver who would be found criminally liable in the event of an offence 'committed' by a car in an automated mode, such as speeding[35] or leaving a vehicle in a dangerous position.[36] Given that such questions have significant potential to disrupt innovation, the industry is likely to welcome statutory guidance.

7.24 There is some criminal regulation in this area already. The General Product Safety Regulations 2005 (GPSR) already provide criminal offences under Regulation 20 in relation to either placing an unsafe product into markets (Regulation 5(1)), or through the distribution and supply of unsafe products (Regulation 8). An offence under this Act could result in a fine of up to £20,000 or 12 months' imprisonment per product. Moreover, the Corporate Manslaughter and Corporate Homicide Act 2007 (CMCHA) makes it an offence to cause a person's death due to a 'gross breach' of the relevant duty of care. Such a breach occurs where the organisation 'falls far below what can reasonably be expected of the organisation in the circumstances'.[37] The 'gross' element is a difficult one to overcome, and the regime has been the subject of criticism because the vast majority of convictions have been around smaller organisations, due to the difficulties in establishing senior management failure at larger corporations.[38] The penalties upon conviction are much more severe than the GPSR, with significant fines.[39]

7.25 Nonetheless, there is a clear gap in coverage between the GPSR and CMCHA in relation to autonomous vehicles, particularly where the vehicle causes serious injury; the damages under the GPSR are insignificant compared with the damages obtained under the CMCHA which only covers death. This is therefore an area which is susceptible to greater discussion and reform in the future.

7.26 Provisions around the Road Traffic Act 1988 with regard to dangerous (Section 2) and careless (Section 3) driving will also need updating due to the reference to a 'person', meaning that situations where a vehicle is in control would not fall within circumstances where a vehicle is itself driving dangerously. Questions will continue to arise around the determination of

35 Section 89 Road Traffic Regulation Act 1984.

36 Section 22 Road Traffic Act 1988.

37 Section 1(4)(B) CMCHA. Matters to be taken into account include: '(a) how serious that failure was; (b) how much of a risk of death it posed' (Section 8(2)). Further, '(a)...attitudes, policies, systems or accepted practices within the organisation that were likely to have encouraged any such failure as is mentioned in subsection (2), or to have produced tolerance of it (b) have regard to any health and safety guidance that relates to the alleged breach' (Section 8 (3)).

38 Sarah Field, 'Ten years on: the Corporate Manslaughter and Corporate Homicide Act 2007: plus ca change?' (2018) International Company and Commercial Law Review 29(8), 511, 516–517.

39 This is unlimited; as noted in ibid., the average fines are around £500,000.

criminal responsibility of the 'driver' in relation to an accident caused by the failure of assisted technology or where the vehicle is in transition, and this is something that will likely need to be regulated for. For example, if a vehicle fails to comply with traffic signs under Section 36 RTA 1988, and the vehicle is of lower automation and therefore only 'assisting' the driver, this may fall into a grey area. Due to the strict liability nature of this provision, there is potential for driver prosecution due to the vehicle breaching this provision, despite the driver not necessarily being at fault for this. Clarification and reform in this area would also be welcome.

Changes to the driving test

7.27 Under current legislation, a person who holds a full category B (car) driving licence is authorised to drive any car. There are no specific requirements beyond this which would be necessary for a driver to operate a highly or fully automated vehicle.

7.28 In the near or medium term, it may well be that the standard driving test is altered to require some familiarity with automated features. Interestingly, in December 2017 the driving test was amended to include following directions from a satellite navigation device, so there is a ready precedent for such a change.[40]

7.29 More radically, in the future there may be some differentiation in the driving test regime. At present, most people sit the full driving test which permits them to drive both automatic and manual vehicles, but there is an option to sit a simpler test to drive automatic vehicles only. It is certainly possible that – technology permitting – an option could be introduced which allows a user to 'drive' *only* a highly automated vehicle.

Changes to the MOT

7.30 An automated vehicle which was more than three years old would require an annual MOT test in the usual way. At present, there are no special standards available for testing such vehicles, behind the existing requirements. However, ultimately it may be that it would be appropriate to specify a more sophisticated MOT to cater for highly or fully automated vehicles. The development of such an MOT would require detailed input from manufacturers and technicians, and is presently some way off.

Mobility as a Service (MaaS)

7.31 Finally, the rise of autonomous vehicles is inherently intertwined with the rise of 'Mobility as a Service'. This term describes a shift away from

---

40 'Driving test changes: 4 December 2017', www.gov.uk/government/news/driving-test-changes-4-december-2017, accessed 30 August 2018.

personally owned modes of transportation and towards mobility solutions that are consumed as a service. Rather than owning their own car, a modern consumer may instead already use 'e-hailing' companies such as Uber or Gett or a car-sharing service such as Zipcar.[41]

7.32 This trend is anticipated to accelerate as autonomous vehicles enter the market. A highly automated car will likely require the regular download of software patches and updates, much like a modern PC. However, unlike a modern PC, failure to carry this out could lead to personal injury. A business model whereby cars are owned by a company and then leased to individuals – or simply summoned on demand – is much more likely to ensure that any necessary patches are made in a timely manner. Such a service would also be potentially more convenient and cheaper for users. Ultimately, we may see the rise of a business model which has been described as 'Uber without drivers'.

41 Consumers owning their own vehicles outright is already increasingly rare. In 2016, 82% of new cars were funded by Personal Contract Payments, a form of hire purchase whereby a large proportion of the vehicle's price is deferred to a final 'balloon payment'. Many consumers chose not to make the final 'balloon payment' and instead return the vehicle in exchange for the use of another new car.

APPENDIX I

ELIZABETH II **c.18**

Automated and Electric Vehicles Act 2018

2018 CHAPTER 18

An Act to make provision about automated vehicles and electric vehicles.

[19th July 2018]

BE IT ENACTED by the Queen's most Excellent Majesty, by and with the advice and consent of the Lords Spiritual and Temporal, and Commons, in this present Parliament assembled, and by the authority of the same, as follows:—

PART 1

AUTOMATED VEHICLES: LIABILITY OF INSURERS ETC

1 Listing of automated vehicles by the Secretary of State

(1) The Secretary of State must prepare, and keep up to date, a list of all motor vehicles that—

(a) are in the Secretary of State's opinion designed or adapted to be capable, in at least some circumstances or situations, of safely driving themselves, and

(b) may lawfully be used when driving themselves, in at least some circumstances or situations, on roads or other public places in Great Britain.

(2) The list may identify vehicles—

(a) by type,

(b) by reference to information recorded in a registration document issued under regulations made under section 22 of the Vehicle Excise and Registration Act 1994, or

(c) in some other way.

(3) The Secretary of State must publish the list when it is first prepared and each time it is revised.

(4) In this Part "automated vehicle" means a vehicle listed under this section.

2 Liability of insurers etc where accident caused by automated vehicle

(1) Where —

(a) an accident is caused by an automated vehicle when driving itself on a road or other public place in Great Britain,

(b) the vehicle is insured at the time of the accident, and

(c) an insured person or any other person suffers damage as a result of the accident,

the insurer is liable for that damage.

(2) Where —

(a) an accident is caused by an automated vehicle when driving itself on a road or other public place in Great Britain,

(b) the vehicle is not insured at the time of the accident,

(c) section 143 of the Road Traffic Act 1988 (users of motor vehicles to be insured or secured against third-party risks) does not apply to the vehicle at that time—

(i) because of section 144(2) of that Act (exemption for public bodies etc), or

(ii) because the vehicle is in the public service of the Crown, and

(d) a person suffers damage as a result of the accident,

the owner of the vehicle is liable for that damage.

(3) In this Part "damage" means death or personal injury, and any damage to property other than—

(a) the automated vehicle,

(b) goods carried for hire or reward in or on that vehicle or in or on any trailer (whether or not coupled) drawn by it, or

(c) property in the custody, or under the control, of—

(i) the insured person (where subsection (1) applies), or

(ii) the person in charge of the automated vehicle at the time of the accident (where subsection (2) applies).

(4) In respect of damage to property caused by, or arising out of, any one accident involving an automated vehicle, the amount of the liability under this section of the insurer or owner of the vehicle is limited to the amount for the time being specified in section 145(4)(b) of the Road Traffic Act 1988 (limit on compulsory insurance for property damage).

(5) This section has effect subject to section 3.

(6) Except as provided by section 4, liability under this section may not be limited or excluded by a term of an insurance policy or in any other way.

(7) The imposition by this section of liability on the insurer or vehicle owner does not affect any other person's liability in respect of the accident.

3 Contributory negligence etc

(1) Where—

(a) an insurer or vehicle owner is liable under section 2 to a person ("the injured party") in respect of an accident, and

(b) the accident, or the damage resulting from it, was to any extent caused by the injured party,

the amount of the liability is subject to whatever reduction under the Law Reform (Contributory Negligence) Act 1945 would apply to a claim in respect of the accident brought by the injured party against a person other than the insurer or vehicle owner.

(2) The insurer or owner of an automated vehicle is not liable under section 2 to the person in charge of the vehicle where the accident that it caused was wholly due to the person's negligence in allowing the vehicle to begin driving itself when it was not appropriate to do so.

4 Accident resulting from unauthorised software alterations or failure to update software

(1) An insurance policy in respect of an automated vehicle may exclude or limit the insurer's liability under section 2(1) for damage suffered by an insured person arising from an accident occurring as a direct result of—

(a) software alterations made by the insured person, or with the insured person's knowledge, that are prohibited under the policy, or

(b) a failure to install safety-critical software updates that the insured person knows, or ought reasonably to know, are safety-critical.

(2) But as regards liability for damage suffered by an insured person who is not the holder of the policy, subsection (1)(a) applies only in relation to software alterations which, at the time of the accident, the person knows are prohibited under the policy.

(3) Subsection (4) applies where an amount is paid by an insurer under section 2(1) in respect of damage suffered, as a result of an accident, by someone who is not insured under the policy in question.

(4) If the accident occurred as a direct result of—

(a) software alterations made by an insured person, or with an insured person's knowledge, that were prohibited under the policy, or

(b) a failure to install safety-critical software updates that an insured person knew, or ought reasonably to have known, were safety-critical,

the amount paid by the insurer is recoverable from that person to the extent provided for by the policy.

(5) But as regards recovery from an insured person who is not the holder of the policy, subsection (4)(a) applies only in relation to software alterations which, at the time of the accident, the person knew were prohibited under the policy.

(6) For the purposes of this section —

(a) "software alterations" and "software updates", in relation to an automated vehicle, mean (respectively) alterations and updates to the vehicle's software;

(b) software updates are "safety-critical" if it would be unsafe to use the vehicle in question without the updates being installed.

5 Right of insurer etc to claim against person responsible for accident

(1) Where—

(a) section 2 imposes on an insurer, or the owner of a vehicle, liability to a person who has suffered damage as a result of an accident ("the injured party"), and

(b) the amount of the insurer's or vehicle owner's liability to the injured party in respect of the accident (including any liability not imposed by section 2) is settled,

any other person liable to the injured party in respect of the accident is under the same liability to the insurer or vehicle owner.

(2) For the purposes of this section, the amount of the insurer's or vehicle owner's liability is settled when it is established—

(a) by a judgment or decree,

(b) by an award in arbitral proceedings or by an arbitration, or

(c) by an enforceable agreement.

(3) If the amount recovered under this section by the insurer or vehicle owner exceeds the amount which that person has agreed or been ordered to pay to the injured party (ignoring so much of either amount as represents interest), the insurer or vehicle owner is liable to the injured party for the difference.

(4) Nothing in this section allows the insurer or vehicle owner and the injured party, between them, to recover from any person more than the amount of that person's liability to the injured party.

(5) For the purposes of—

(a) section 10A of the Limitation Act 1980 (special time limit for actions by insurers etc in respect of automated vehicles), or

(b) section 18ZC of the Prescription and Limitation (Scotland) Act 1973 (actions under this section),

the right of action that an insurer or vehicle owner has by virtue of this section accrues at the time of the settlement referred to in subsection (1)(b).

6 Application of enactments

(1) Any damage for which a person is liable under section 2 is treated as if it had been caused—

(a) for the purposes of the Fatal Accidents Act 1976, by that person's wrongful act, neglect or default;

(b) for the purposes of sections 3 to 6 of the Damages (Scotland) Act 2011 (asp 7) (rights of relatives of a deceased), by that person's act or omission;

(c) for the purposes of Part 2 of the Administration of Justice Act 1982 (damages for personal injuries, etc Scotland), by an act or omission giving rise to liability in that person to pay damages.

(2) Section 1 of the Congenital Disabilities (Civil Liability) Act 1976 ("the 1976 Act") has effect for the purposes of section 2 of this Act—

(a) as if a person were answerable to a child in respect of an accident caused by an automated vehicle when driving itself if the person—

(i) is or has been liable under section 2 in respect of any effect of the accident on a parent of the child, or

(ii) would be so liable if the accident caused a parent of the child to suffer damage;

(b) as if the provisions of this Part relating to liability under section 2 applied in relation to liability by virtue of paragraph (a) above under section 1 of the 1976 Act;

(c) as if subsection (6) of section 1 of the 1976 Act (exclusion of liability) were omitted.

(3) For the purposes of section 3(1), the Law Reform (Contributory Negligence) Act 1945 and section 5 of the Fatal Accidents Act 1976 (contributory negligence) have effect as if the behaviour of the automated vehicle were the fault of the person made liable for the damage by section 2 of this Act.

(4) Liability under section 2 is treated as liability in tort or, in Scotland, delict for the purposes of any enactment conferring jurisdiction on a court with respect to any matter.

(5) An insurer or vehicle owner who has a right of action against a person by virtue of section 5 does not have a right to recover contribution from that person under the Civil Liability (Contribution) Act 1978 or under section 3 of the Law Reform (Miscellaneous Provisions) (Scotland) Act 1940.

7 Report by Secretary of State on operation of this Part

(1) The Secretary of State must prepare a report assessing—

(a) the impact and effectiveness of section 1;

(b) the extent to which the provisions of this Part ensure that appropriate insurance or other arrangements are made in respect of vehicles that are capable of safely driving themselves.

(2) The report must be laid before Parliament no later than two years after the first publication of the list under section 1.

8 Interpretation

(1) For the purposes of this Part—

(a) a vehicle is "driving itself" if it is operating in a mode in which it is not being controlled, and does not need to be monitored, by an individual;

(b) a vehicle is "insured" if there is in force in relation to the use of the vehicle on a road or other public place in Great Britain a policy of insurance that satisfies the conditions in section 145 of the Road Traffic Act 1988.

(2) In this Part—

"automated vehicle" has the meaning given by section 1(4); "damage" has the meaning given by section 2(3);

"insured person", in relation to an insured vehicle, means any person whose use of the vehicle is covered by the policy in question;

"insurer", in relation to an insured vehicle, means the insurer under that policy;

"road" has the same meaning as in the Road Traffic Act 1988 (see section 192(1) of that Act).

(3) In this Part—

(a) a reference to an accident includes a reference to two or more causally related accidents;

(b) a reference to an accident caused by an automated vehicle includes a reference to an accident that is partly caused by an automated vehicle.

PART 2

ELECTRIC VEHICLES: CHARGING

Introductory

9 Definitions

(1) For the purposes of this Part—

(a) "charge point" means a device intended for charging a vehicle that is capable of being propelled by electrical power derived from a storage battery (or for discharging electricity stored in such a vehicle);

(b) "hydrogen refuelling point" means a device intended for refuelling a vehicle that is capable of being propelled by electrical power derived from hydrogen;

(c) a charge point or a hydrogen refuelling point is a "public charging or refuelling point" if it is provided for use by members of the general public.

(2) In this Part—

"operator", in relation to a public charging or refuelling point, has the meaning given by regulations;

"prescribed" means prescribed by regulations;

"vehicle" means a vehicle that is intended or adapted for use on roads.

Requirements and prohibitions

10 Public charging or refuelling points: access, standards and connection

(1) Regulations may impose requirements on operators of public charging or refuelling points in connection with—

(a) the method of payment or other way by which access to the use of public charging or refuelling points may be obtained;

(b) performance, maintenance and availability of public charging or refuelling points;

(c) the components of public charging or refuelling points that provide the means by which vehicles connect to such points ("connecting components").

(2) Regulations under subsection (1)(a) may require operators—

(a) to provide a prescribed method of payment or verification for obtaining access to the use of public charging or refuelling points;

(b) to co-operate with each other for the purposes of a requirement imposed by the regulations (for example, by sharing facilities or information);

(c) to take prescribed steps for the purposes of such a requirement (for example, to provide information to a prescribed person).

(3) Regulations under subsection (1)(b) may, for example, require the operator of a public charging or refuelling point to ensure that the point complies with prescribed requirements (which may include technical specifications).

(4) Regulations under subsection (1)(c) may, for example, require the operator of a public charging or refuelling point to ensure that its connecting components comply with prescribed requirements (which may include technical specifications for connecting components or any related equipment).

11 Large fuel retailers etc: provision of public charging or refuelling points

(1) Regulations may impose requirements on—

(a) large fuel retailers falling within a prescribed description, or

(b) service area operators falling within a prescribed description,

in connection with the provision on their premises of public charging or refuelling points.

(2) Regulations under subsection (1) may, for example—

(a) require large fuel retailers or service area operators to provide public charging or refuelling points;

(b) require public charging or refuelling points to be available for use at prescribed times;

(c) require services or facilities prescribed by the regulations to be provided in connection with public charging or refuelling points.

(3) In this section "large fuel retailer" and "service area operator" have the meaning given by regulations.

12 Duty to consider making regulations under section 11(1)(a) on request by elected mayor

(1) The Secretary of State must consider making section 11(1)(a) regulations in relation to the whole or part of a relevant area if—

(a) the mayor for the relevant area makes a request for such regulations to be made,

(b) conditions 1 to 3 are met, and

(c) the Secretary of State considers that the mayor has complied with any prescribed requirements before making the request.

(2) "Section 11(1)(a) regulations" means regulations under section 11(1) that impose requirements on large fuel retailers within section 11(1)(a).

(3) Condition 1 is that the Secretary of State is satisfied that, before making the request, the mayor—

(a) published proposals for section 11(1)(a) regulations to be made in relation to the whole or part of the relevant area, and

(b) consulted—

(i) each local authority any part of whose area falls within the relevant area or, if the request relates to part of the relevant area, within that part,

(ii) persons who would be likely to be subject to requirements under the regulations (if made), and

(iii) such other persons as the mayor considers appropriate,

in relation to the published proposals.

(4) Condition 2 is that the mayor has given the Secretary of State a summary of the responses to the consultation referred to in subsection (3)(b).

(5) Condition 3 is that regulations have been made under section 11(3) in relation to the meaning of "large fuel retailer".

(6) If the Secretary of State decides not to make section 11(1)(a) regulations in response to the mayor's request, the Secretary of State must notify the mayor of the decision and the reasons for it.

(7) For the purposes of this section—

(a) "relevant area" means the area of a combined authority or Greater London;

(b) the mayor for a relevant area is—

(i) in the case of the area of a combined authority, the mayor for the area elected in accordance with section 107A(2) of the 2009 Act;

(ii) in the case of Greater London, the Mayor of London.

(8) In this section—

"the 2009 Act" means the Local Democracy, Economic Development and Construction Act 2009;

"combined authority" means a combined authority established under section 103(1) of the 2009 Act;

"large fuel retailer" has the same meaning as in section 11; "local authority" means—

(a) a district council,
(b) a county council, or
(c) a London borough council.

13 Information for users of public charging or refuelling points

(1) Regulations may require operators of public charging or refuelling points to make available prescribed information relating to such points.

(2) The information that may be prescribed under subsection (1) in relation to a public charging or refuelling point is such information as the Secretary of State considers likely to be useful to users or potential users of the point, for example information about—

(a) the location of the point and its operating hours,
(b) available charging or refuelling options,
(c) the cost of obtaining access to the use of the point,
(d) the method of payment or other way by which access to the use of the point may be obtained,
(e) means of connection to the point,
(f) whether the point is in working order, and
(g) whether the point is in use.

(3) The regulations may make provision—

(a) about when, how, to whom and in what form the information is to be made available;
(b) for the information to be made available without restrictions on its use and disclosure.

(4) The regulations may be made so as to have effect for a prescribed period.

14 Transmission of data relating to charge points

(1) Regulations may make provision for the purpose of ensuring the ongoing transmission of charge point data to a prescribed person or to persons of a prescribed description.

(2) "Charge point data" means prescribed information relating to a charge point (which may include information about energy consumption and geographical information).

(3) Regulations under subsection (1) may impose requirements—

(a) on operators of charge points that are provided for use by members of the general public, and
(b) in relation to charge points that are not provided as mentioned in paragraph (a), on prescribed persons or persons of a prescribed description (subject to subsection (4)).

(4) Regulations under subsection (1) may not impose requirements on owners or occupiers of domestic premises.

(5) Regulations under subsection (1) may make provision about when, how and in what form charge point data is to be transmitted.

15 Smart charge points

(1) Regulations may provide that a person must not sell or install a charge point unless it complies with prescribed requirements.

(2) The requirements that may be imposed under subsection (1) include requirements relating to the technical specifications for a charge point, including for example the ability of a charge point—

(a) to receive and process information provided by a prescribed person,

(b) to react to information of a kind mentioned in paragraph (a) (for example, by adjusting the rate of charging or discharging),

(c) to transmit information (including geographical information) to a prescribed person,

(d) to monitor and record energy consumption,

(e) to comply with requirements relating to security,

(f) to achieve energy efficiency, and

(g) to be accessed remotely.

(3) Regulations under subsection (1) may also prescribe requirements to be met in relation to the sale or installation of a charge point.

(4) In this section—

(a) "sell" includes let on hire, lend or give;

(b) references to a prescribed person include references to—

(i) a person of a prescribed description, and

(ii) a device operated by one or more prescribed persons.

General and supplementary

16 Enforcement

(1) Regulations under this Part may make provision for enforcement in connection with a contravention of a requirement or prohibition imposed by the regulations.

(2) Regulations made by virtue of subsection (1) may, for example—

(a) contain provision for determining whether there has been a failure to comply with a requirement or prohibition;

(b) provide for the imposition of a financial penalty (and for the payment of such a penalty into the Consolidated Fund);

(c) set out the procedure to be followed in imposing a penalty;

(d) make provision about the amount of a penalty;

(e) make provision about the enforcement of a penalty;

(f) provide for a right of appeal against the imposition of a penalty;

(g) provide for a determination for the purposes of the regulations to be made by the Secretary of State or a prescribed person.

(3) The provision referred to in subsection (2)(a) includes—

(a) provision authorising a prescribed person to enter any land in accordance with the regulations;

(b) provision for the inspection or testing of any thing by a prescribed person, which may for example include provision about—

(i) the production of documents or other things,

(ii) the provision of information,

(iii) the making of photographs or copies, and
(iv) the removal of any thing for the purpose of inspection or testing and its retention for that purpose for a reasonable period.

17 Exceptions

(1) Regulations under this Part may create exceptions from any requirement or prohibition imposed by the regulations.
(2) An exception may be created in relation to a prescribed description of persons or devices.
(3) The Secretary of State may determine that a requirement or prohibition imposed by regulations under this Part does not apply in relation to a person or device specified in the determination.
(4) The Secretary of State must publish a determination made under subsection (3).

18 Regulations

(1) Regulations under this Part—
(a) may make different provision for different purposes or different areas;
(b) may make supplemental, incidental, transitional or consequential provision.
(2) A power to make regulations under this Part is exercisable by the Secretary of State by statutory instrument.
(3) Before making regulations under this Part, the Secretary of State must consult such persons as the Secretary of State considers appropriate.
(4) Subject to subsection (7), where —
(a) a statutory instrument contains regulations under this Part, and
(b) any of those regulations are the first regulations under a provision of this Part, the instrument may not be made unless a draft of it has been laid before Parliament and approved by a resolution of each House.
(5) Where —
(a) a statutory instrument contains regulations under section 11 (large fuel retailers etc), and
(b) the regulations amend the definition of "large fuel retailer" or "service area operator", the instrument containing the regulations may not be made unless a draft of it has been laid before Parliament and approved by a resolution of each House.
(6) A statutory instrument containing regulations under this Part none of which are—
(a) the first regulations under a provision of this Part, or
(b) regulations to which subsection (5) applies, is subject to annulment in pursuance of a resolution of either House of Parliament.
(7) Where regulations contain only provision made by virtue of—
(a) section 10(3) or (4) (prescribed requirements for public charging or refuelling points or for connecting components), or
(b) section 15 (prescribed requirements for charge points), the instrument containing the regulations is subject to annulment in pursuance of a resolution of either House of Parliament.
(8) If a draft of a statutory instrument containing relevant section 11(1)(a) regulations would, apart from this subsection, be treated for the purposes of the

standing orders of either House of Parliament as a hybrid instrument, it is to proceed in that House as if it were not such an instrument.

(9) In subsection (8) "relevant section 11(1)(a) regulations" means regulations under section 11(1)(a) that are made pursuant to section 12 (duty to consider making regulations under section 11(1)(a) on request by elected mayor).

19 Report by Secretary of State on operation of this Part

(1) The Secretary of State must, in respect of each reporting period, prepare a report assessing—

(a) the impact and effectiveness of regulations made under this Part;

(b) the need for regulations to be made under this Part during subsequent reporting periods.

(2) Each report must be laid before Parliament after the end of the reporting period to which it relates.

(3) The first reporting period is the period of two years beginning with the day on which this Act is passed.

(4) Each subsequent period of 12 months after the first reporting period is a reporting period.

PART 3

MISCELLANEOUS AND GENERAL

20 Minor and consequential amendments

(1) The Schedule (minor and consequential amendments) has effect.

(2) The Secretary of State may by regulations make provision that is consequential on any provision made by this Act.

(3) The power to make regulations under this section is exercisable by statutory instrument.

(4) Regulations under this section may amend any enactment passed or made before this Act or in the same Session.

(5) A statutory instrument containing regulations under this section any of which amend primary legislation may not be made unless a draft of the instrument has been laid before Parliament and approved by a resolution of each House.

(6) A statutory instrument containing regulations under this section none of which amends primary legislation is subject to annulment in pursuance of a resolution of either House of Parliament.

(7) In this section—

"amend" includes repeal or revoke;

"primary legislation" means—

(a) an Act of Parliament;

(b) an Act of the Scottish Parliament;

(c) an Act or Measure of the National Assembly for Wales;

(d) Northern Ireland legislation.

21 Commencement

(1) This Act comes into force on whatever day or days the Secretary of State appoints by regulations.

(2) Subsection (1) does not apply to the following provisions of this Act (which come into force on the day on which this Act is passed)—
 (a) section 20(2) to (7);
 (b) this section;
 (c) sections 22 and 23.
(3) The power to make regulations under this section is exercisable by statutory instrument.
(4) Regulations under this section—
 (a) may appoint different days for different purposes or different areas;
 (b) may make transitional, transitory or saving provision.

22 Extent

(1) Part 1 extends to England and Wales and Scotland.
(2) Part 2 extends to England and Wales, Scotland and Northern Ireland.
(3) An amendment made by the Schedule has the same extent as the provision to which it relates.

23 Short title

This Act may be cited as the Automated and Electric Vehicles Act 2018.

SCHEDULE

Minor and consequential amendments

Prescription and Limitation (Scotland) Act 1973 (c. 52)

(1) In section 17 of the Prescription and Limitation (Scotland) Act 1973 (actions in respect of personal injuries not resulting in death), after subsection (1) insert—
 "(1A) This section does not apply to an action of damages in respect of personal injuries to which section 18ZA applies."
(2) In section 18 of that Act (actions where death has resulted from personal injuries), after subsection (1) insert—
 "(1A) This section does not apply to an action of damages in respect of personal injuries or death to which section 18ZA applies."
(3) After that section insert—

"18ZA Actions under section 2 of the Automated and Electric Vehicles Act 2018

(1) This section applies to an action of damages under section 2 of the 2018 Act (liability of insurers etc where accident caused by automated vehicle).
(2) An action may not be brought after the expiry of the period of 3 years beginning with—
 (a) the date of the accident mentioned in subsection (1) or (as the case may be) subsection (2) of that section, or
 (b) where subsection (3) applies, the date on which the person who sustained the injuries first became aware of the facts mentioned in subsection (4) (if later).

(3) This subsection applies where the damages claimed consist of or include damages in respect of personal injuries (to the pursuer or any other person).

(4) The facts are—

(a) that the injury in question was significant;

(b) that the injury was attributable in whole or in part to an accident caused by an automated vehicle when driving itself; and

(c) the identity of the insurer of the vehicle (in the case of an action under section 2(1) of the 2018 Act) or the owner of the vehicle (in the case of an action under section 2(2) of that Act).

(5) Expressions used in subsection (4) that are defined for the purposes of Part 1 of the 2018 Act have the same meaning in that subsection as in that Part.

(6) In the computation of the period specified in subsection (2) above any time during which the person who sustained the injuries was under legal disability by reason of nonage or unsoundness of mind is to be disregarded.

(7) If a person injured in the accident dies before the expiry of the period mentioned in subsection (2) above, an action may not be brought after the expiry of the period of 3 years beginning with—

(a) the date of death of the person, or

(b) where subsection (3) applies, the date on which the pursuer first became aware of the facts mentioned in subsection (4) (if later).

(8) Where an action has not been brought before the expiry of the period mentioned in subsection (2) above and the person subsequently dies in consequence of injuries sustained in the accident, an action may not be brought in respect of those injuries or that death.

(9) Subsection (10) applies if a person injured in the accident dies and the person seeking to bring the action is a relative of the deceased.

(10) In the computation of the period specified in subsection (7) any time during which the relative was under legal disability by reason of nonage or unsoundness of mind is to be disregarded.

(11) In this section—

"the 2018 Act" means the Automated and Electric Vehicles Act 2018;

"relative" has the same meaning as in the Damages (Scotland) Act 2011.

18ZB Section 18ZA: extension of limitation periods

(1) Subsection (2) applies where a person would be entitled, but for section 18ZA, to bring an action other than one in which the damages claimed are confined to damages for loss of or damage to property.

(2) The court may, if it seems to it equitable to do so, allow the person to bring the action despite that section.

18ZC Actions under section 5 of the Automated and Electric Vehicles Act 2018

(1) Subsection (2) applies where, by virtue of section 5 of the Automated and Electric Vehicles Act 2018 (right of insurer etc to claim against person responsible for accident), an insurer or vehicle owner becomes entitled to bring an action against any person.

(2) The action may not be brought after the expiry of the period of 2 years beginning with the date on which the right of action accrued (under subsection (5) of that section)."

(4) In section 19CA of that Act (interruption of limitation period: arbitration), in subsection (1), after "18(2)," insert "18ZA(2) or (7), 18ZC(2),".

(5) In section 19F of that Act (extension of limitation periods: cross-border mediation), in subsection (1), after "18," insert "18ZA, 18ZC,".

(6) In section 22 of that Act (interpretation of Part 2 and supplementary provisions), in subsection (2)—

(a) for "or 18A" substitute ", 18A or 18ZA";

(b) after "the said section 18A" insert "or subsection (3) or (7)(b) of the said section 18ZA".

(7) In Schedule 1 to that Act (obligations affected by prescriptive periods of 5 years under section 6), in paragraph 2, after sub-paragraph (g) insert—

"(ga) to any obligation to make reparation arising from liability under section 2 of the Automated and Electric Vehicles Act 2018 (liability of insurer etc. where accident caused by automated vehicle);".

Limitation Act 1980 (c. 58)

(8) In section 9 of the Limitation Act 1980 (time limit for actions for sums recoverable by statute), in subsection (2), after "section 10" insert "or 10A".

(9) After section 10 of that Act insert—

"10A Special time limit for actions by insurers etc in respect of automated vehicles

(1) Where by virtue of section 5 of the Automated and Electric Vehicles Act 2018 an insurer or vehicle owner becomes entitled to bring an action against any person, the action shall not be brought after the expiration of two years from the date on which the right of action accrued (under subsection (5) of that section).

(2) An action referred to in subsection (1) shall be one to which sections 32, 33A and 35 of this Act apply, but otherwise Parts 2 and 3 of this Act (except sections 37 and 38) shall not apply for the purposes of this section."

(10) In the italic heading before section 11 of that Act, after "personal injuries or death" insert "etc".

(11) After section 11A of that Act insert—

"11B Actions against insurers etc of automated vehicles

(1) None of the time limits given in the preceding provisions of this Act shall apply to an action for damages under section 2 of the Automated and Electric Vehicles Act 2018 (liability of insurer etc where accident caused by automated vehicle).

But this subsection does not affect the application of section 5A of this Act.

(2) An action for damages against an insurer under subsection (1) of section 2 of the Automated and Electric Vehicles Act 2018 (including an action by an insured person under a contract of insurance in respect of the insurer's obligations under that section) shall not be brought after the expiration of the period of three years from—

(a) the date of the accident referred to in that subsection; or

(b) where subsection (3) below applies, the date of knowledge of the person injured (if later).

(3) This subsection applies where the damages claimed consist of or include damages in respect of personal injuries (to the claimant or any other person).

(4) An action for damages against the owner of a vehicle under subsection (2) of that section shall not be brought after the expiration of the period of three years from—

(a) the date of the accident referred to in that subsection; or

(b) where subsection (3) above applies, the date of knowledge of the person injured (if later).

(5) If a person injured in the accident dies before the expiration of the period mentioned in subsection (2) or (4) above, the period applicable as respects the cause of action surviving for the benefit of the person's estate by virtue of section 1 of the Law Reform (Miscellaneous Provisions) Act 1934 shall be three years from—

(a) the date of death; or

(b) where subsection (3) above applies, the date of the personal representative's knowledge (if later).

(6) If there is more than one personal representative, and their dates of knowledge are different, subsection (5)(b) above shall be read as referring to the earliest of those dates.

(7) In this section "personal representative" has the same meaning as in section 11 of this Act."

(12) In section 12 of that Act (special time limit for actions under Fatal Accidents legislation), in subsection (1), for "or 11A" substitute ", 11A or 11B".

(13) (1) Section 14 of that Act (definition of date of knowledge for purposes of sections 11 and 12) is amended as follows.

(2) In the heading, for "sections 11 and 12" substitute "sections 11 to 12".

(3) In subsection (1), for "subsection (1A)" substitute "subsections (1A) and (1B)".

(4) After subsection (1A) insert—

"(1B) In section 11B of this Act and in section 12 of this Act so far as that section applies to an action by virtue of section 6(1)(a) of the Automated and Electric Vehicles Act 2018 ("the 2018 Act") (death caused by automated vehicle) references to a person's date of knowledge are references to the date on which he first had knowledge of the following facts—

(a) that the injury in question was significant; and

(b) that the injury was attributable in whole or in part to an accident caused by an automated vehicle when driving itself; and

(c) the identity of the insurer of the vehicle (in the case of an action under section 2(1) of the 2018 Act) or the owner of the vehicle (in the case of an action under section 2(2) of that Act).

Expressions used in this subsection that are defined for the purposes of Part 1 of the 2018 Act have the same meaning in this subsection as in that Part."

(14) In section 28 of that Act (extension of limitation period in case of disability), in subsection (6), after "section 11" insert ", 11B".

(15) (1) Section 32 of that Act (postponement of limitation period in case of concealment etc) is amended as follows.

(2) In subsection (1), for "and (4A)" substitute ", (4A) and (4B)".

(3) After subsection (4A) insert—

"(4B) Subsection (1) above shall not apply in relation to the time limit prescribed by section 11B(2) or (4) of this Act or in relation to that time limit as applied by virtue of section 12(1) of this Act."

(16) (1) Section 33 of that Act (discretionary exclusion of time limit) is amended as follows.

(2) In subsection (1), in paragraph (a), for "or 11A" substitute ", 11A, 11B".

(3) After subsection (1A) insert—

"(1B) Where the damages claimed are confined to damages for loss of or damage to any property, the court shall not under this section disapply any provision in its application to an action under section 2 of the Automated and Electric Vehicles Act 2018."

(4) In subsections (2) and (4), for "or subsection (4) of section 11A" substitute ", 11A(4) or 11B(2) or (4)".

(5) In subsection (3)(b), after "section 11A" insert ", by section 11B".

(6) In subsection (8), for "or 11A" substitute ", 11A or 11B".

Road Traffic Act 1988 (c. 52)

(17) In section 143 of the Road Traffic Act 1988 (users of motor vehicles to be insured or secured against third-party risks), after subsection (1) insert—

"(1A) In the application of this Part to automated vehicles—

(a) subsection (1) above has effect with the omission of the words "or such a security in respect of third party risks" in paragraphs (a) and (b);

(b) this Part has effect with the omission of sections 146 and 147(2);

(c) any other references to a security or certificate of security in this Act are to be ignored."

(18) In section 144 of that Act (exceptions from requirement of third-party insurance etc), in subsection (1), after "does not apply to a vehicle" insert ", other than an automated vehicle,".

(19) (1) Section 145 of that Act (requirements in respect of policies of insurance) is amended as follows.

(2) After subsection (3) insert—

"(3A) In the case of an automated vehicle, the policy must also provide for the insurer's obligations to an insured person under section 2(1) of the Automated and Electric Vehicles Act 2018 (liability of insurers etc.

where accident caused by automated vehicle) to be obligations under the policy.

In this subsection "insured person" means a person who is covered under the policy for using the vehicle on a road or public place in Great Britain."

(3) At the end of subsection (4) insert—

"Paragraph (a) does not apply where the vehicle in question is an automated vehicle."

(20) In section 161 of that Act (interpretation), in subsection (1), at the appropriate place insert—

""automated vehicle" means a vehicle listed by the Secretary of State under section 1 of the Automated and Electric Vehicles Act 2018,".

(21) In section 162 of that Act (index to Part 6), at the appropriate place in the table insert—

"Automated vehicle section 161(1)".

APPENDIX II

The key principles of vehicle cyber security for connected and automated vehicles

Introduction

As vehicles get smarter, cyber security in the automotive industry is becoming an increasing concern. Whether we're turning cars into wifi connected hotspots or equipping them with millions of lines of code to create fully autonomous vehicles, cars are more vulnerable than ever to hacking and data theft.

It's essential that all parties involved in the manufacturing supply chain, from designers and engineers, to retailers and senior level executives, are provided with a consistent set of guidelines that support this global industry. The Department for Transport, in conjunction with Centre for the Protection of National Infrastructure (CPNI), have created the following key principles for use throughout the automotive sector, the CAV and ITS ecosystems and their supply chains.

Principle 1 – Organisational security is owned, governed and promoted at board level

Principle 1.1

There is a security program which is aligned with an organisation's broader mission and objectives.

Principle 1.2

Personal accountability is held at the board level for product and system security (physical, personnel and cyber) and delegated appropriately and clearly throughout the organisation.

Principle 1.3

Awareness and training is implemented to embed a 'culture of security' to ensure individuals understand their role and responsibility in ITS/CAV system security.

Principle 1.4

All new designs embrace security by design. Secure design principles are followed in developing a secure ITS/CAV system, and all aspects of security (physical, personnel and cyber) are integrated into the product and service development process.

Principle 2 – security risks are assessed and managed appropriately and proportionately, including those specific to the supply chain

Principle 2.1

Organisations must require knowledge and understanding of current and relevant threats and the engineering practices to mitigate them in their engineering roles.

Principle 2.2

Organisations collaborate and engage with appropriate third parties to enhance threat awareness and appropriate response planning.

Principle 2.3

Security risk assessment and management procedures are in place within the organisation. Appropriate processes for identification, categorisation, prioritisation, and treatment of security risks, including those from cyber, are developed.

Principle 2.4

Security risks specific to, and/or encompassing, supply chains, sub-contractors and service providers are identified and managed through design, specification and procurement practices.

Principle 3 – organisations need product aftercare and incident response to ensure systems are secure over their lifetime

Principle 3.1

Organisations plan for how to maintain security over the lifetime of their systems, including any necessary after-sales support services.

Principle 3.2

Incident response plans are in place. Organisations plan for how to respond to potential compromise of safety critical assets, non-safety critical assets, and system malfunctions, and how to return affected systems to a safe and secure state.

Principle 3.3

There is an active programme in place to identify critical vulnerabilities and appropriate systems in place to mitigate them in a proportionate manner.

Principle 3.4

Organisations ensure their systems are able to support data forensics and the recovery of forensically robust, uniquely identifiable data. This may be used to identify the cause of any cyber, or other, incident.

Principle 4 – all organisations, including sub-contractors, suppliers and potential 3rd parties, work together to enhance the security of the system

Principle 4.1

Organisations, including suppliers and 3rd parties, must be able to provide assurance, such as independent validation or certification, of their security processes and products (physical, personnel and cyber).

Principle 4.2

It is possible to ascertain and validate the authenticity and origin of all supplies within the supply chain.

Principle 4.3

Organisations jointly plan for how systems will safely and securely interact with external devices, connections (including the ecosystem), services (including maintenance), operations or control centres. This may include agreeing standards and data requirements.

Principle 4.4

Organisations identify and manage external dependencies. Where the accuracy or availability of sensor or external data is critical to automated functions, secondary measures must also be employed.

Principle 5 – systems are designed using a defence-in-depth approach

Principle 5.1

The security of the system does not rely on single points of failure, security by obscuration or anything which cannot be readily changed, should it be compromised.

Principle 5.2

The security architecture applies defence-in-depth and segmented techniques, seeking to mitigate risks with complementary controls such as monitoring, alerting, segregation, reducing attack surfaces (such as open internet ports), trust layers / boundaries and other security protocols.

Principle 5.3

Design controls to mediate transactions across trust boundaries, must be in place throughout the system. These include the least access principle, one-way data controls, full disk encryption and minimising shared data storage.

Principle 5.4

Remote and back-end systems, including cloud based servers, which might provide access to a system have appropriate levels of protection and monitoring in place to prevent unauthorised access.

Principle 6 – The security of all software is managed throughout its lifetime

Principle 6.1

Organisations adopt secure coding practices to proportionately manage risks from known and unknown vulnerabilities in software, including existing code libraries. Systems to manage, audit and test code are in place.

Principle 6.2

It must be possible to ascertain the status of all software, firmware and their configuration, including the version, revision and configuration data of all software components.

Principle 6.3

It's possible to safely and securely update software and return it to a known good state if it becomes corrupt.

Principle 6.4

Software adopts open design practices and peer reviewed code is used where possible. Source code is able to be shared where appropriate.

Principle 7 – The storage and transmission of data is secure and can be controlled

Principle 7.1

Data must be sufficiently secure (confidentiality and integrity) when stored and transmitted so that only the intended recipient or system functions are able to receive and / or access it. Incoming communications are treated as unsecure until validated.

Principle 7.2

Personally identifiable data must be managed appropriately.
This includes:

- what is stored (both on and off the ITS / CAV system)
- what is transmitted
- how it is used
- the control the data owner has over these processes

Where possible, data that is sent to other systems is sanitised.

Principle 7.3

Users are able to delete sensitive data held on systems and connected systems.

Principle 8 – The system is designed to be resilient to attacks and respond appropriately when its defences or sensors fail

Principle 8.1

The system must be able to withstand receiving corrupt, invalid or malicious data or commands via its external and internal interfaces while remaining available for primary use. This includes sensor jamming or spoofing.

Principle 8.2

Systems are resilient and fail-safe if safety-critical functions are compromised or cease to work. The mechanism is proportionate to the risk. The systems are able to respond appropriately if non-safety critical functions fail.

Troubleshooting: applicable standards and guidance

This list is not intended to be exhaustive. Further standards and guidance may be applicable. It's recommended that for specific technologies or processes corporations should check for any applicable standards or guidance that might be of relevance and for any new standards that have been developed in the field.

SAE

- J3061 - Cybersecurity guidebook for cyber-physical vehicle systems
- J3101 - Requirements for hardware protected security for ground vehicle applications

ISO

- 9797–1 – Security techniques: message authentication codes – specifies a model for secure message authentication codes using block cyphers and asymmetric keys
- 12207 – Systems and software engineering – software lifecycle processes
- 15408 – Evaluation of IT security – specifies a model for evaluating security aspects within IT
- 27001 – Information security management system
- 27002 – Code of practice – security – provides recommendations for information management (contains guidance on access control, cryptography and supplier relationship)
- 27010 – Information security management for inter-sector and inter-organizational communications
- 27018 – Code of practice – handling PII / SPI (privacy) – protection of personally identifiable information (PII) in public clouds
- 27034 – Application security techniques – guidance to ensure software delivers necessary level of security in support of an organisations security management system

- 27035 – Information security incident management
- 29101 – Privacy architecture framework
- 29119 – Software testing standard

DEFSTAN

- 05–138 – Cyber security for defence suppliers

NIST

- 800–30 – Guide for conducting risk assessments
- 800–88 – Guidelines for media sanitization
- SP 800–50 – Building an information technology security awareness and training program
- SP 800–61 – Computer security incident handling guide

Other

- Microsoft security development lifecycle (SDL)
- SAFE Code best practices
- OWASP Comprehensive, lightweight application security process (CLASP)
- HMG Security policy framework
- PAS 1192–5 – BSI publication on security-minded building information modelling, digital built environments and smart asset management
- PAS 754 – BSI publication on software trustworthiness, governance and management

APPENDIX III

Levels of vehicle automation[1]

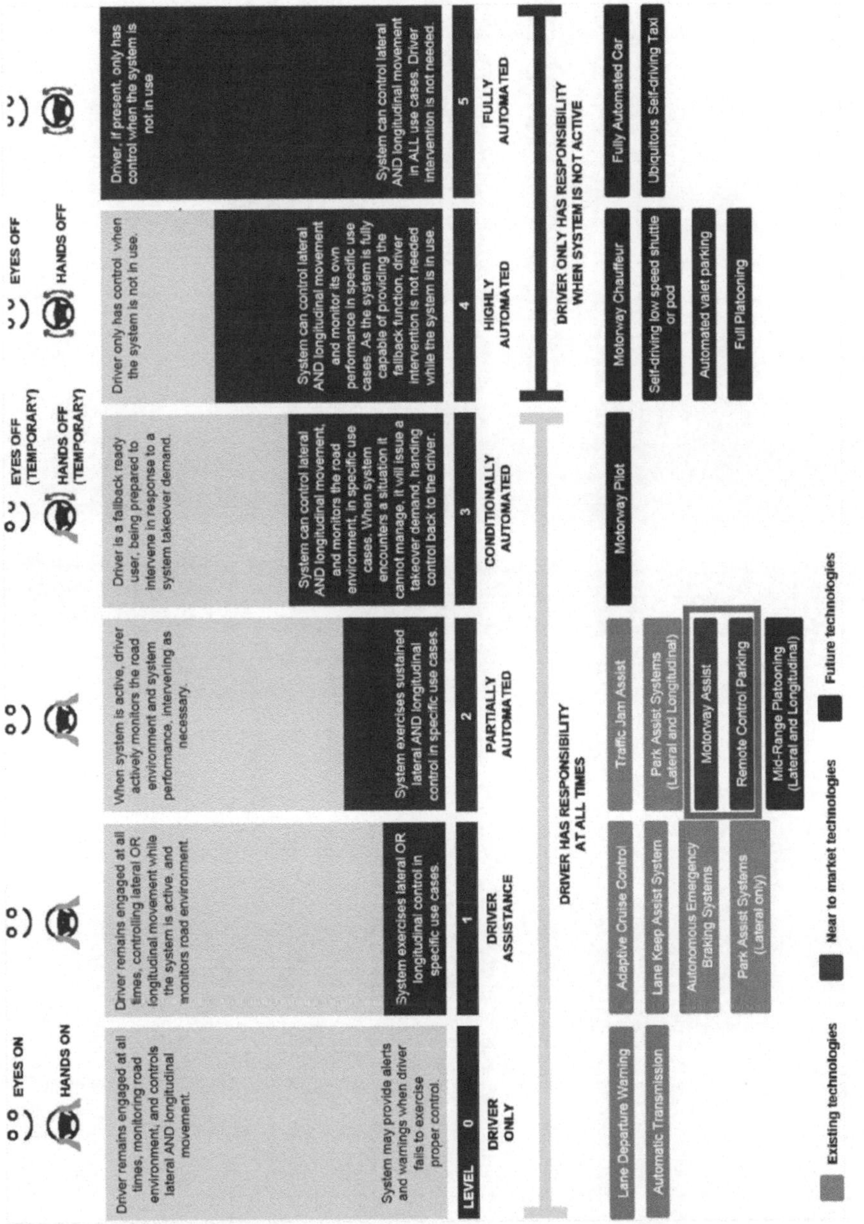

1 This infographic, produced by the Centre for Connected and Autonomous Vehicles, is adapted from the Society of Automotive Engineers J3016 Standard "Taxonomy and Definitions for Terms Related to On-Road Motor Vehicle Automated Driving Systems" (http://standards.sae.org/j3016_201609/). Although SAE J3016 defines a useful means of understanding the different "levels" of vehicle automation, they are not formally recognised by the UK, or the UN bodies responsible for vehicle construction regulations and international road traffic rules.

INDEX